DATE DUE			

**BIO
BROOKS**

33577000671501
Hill, Christine M.

**Gwendolyn Brooks :
"poetry is life
distilled"**

GWENDOLYN BROOKS

"Poetry Is Life Distilled"

Christine M. Hill

Series Consultant:
Dr. Russell L. Adams, Chairman
Department of
Afro-American Studies,
Howard University

E **Enslow Publishers, Inc.**

40 Industrial Road   PO Box 38
Box 398   Aldershot
Berkeley Heights, NJ 07922   Hants GU12 6BP
USA   UK

http://www.enslow.com

"WRITING IS A DELICIOUS AGONY. POETRY IS LIFE DISTILLED."

—Gwendolyn Brooks

Library of Congress Cataloging-in-Publication Data

Hill, Christine M.
    Gwendolyn Brooks : "poetry is life distilled" / Christine M. Hill.
      p. cm. — (African-American biography library)
    Includes bibliographical references and index.
    ISBN-10: 0-7660-2292-7 (hardcover)
    1. Brooks, Gwendolyn, 1917–   . —Juvenile literature. 2. Poets, American—
20th century—Biography—Juvenile literature. 3. African American poets—Biography—
Juvenile literature. 4. Chicago (Ill.)—Biography—Juvenile literature. I. Title. II. Series.
    PS3503.R7244Z68 2005
    811'.54—dc22

                                              2004016801

ISBN-13: 978-0-7660-2292-8

Printed in the United States of America

10 9 8 7 6 5 4 3

To Our Readers:
We have done our best to make sure all Internet Addresses in this book were active and appropriate when we went to press. However, the author and the publisher have no control over and assume no liability for the material available on those Internet sites or on other Web sites they may link to. Any comments or suggestions can be sent by e-mail to comments@enslow.com or to the address on the back cover.

Every effort has been made to locate all copyright holders of material used in this book. If any errors or omissions have occurred, corrections will be made in future editions of this book.

Illustration Credits: AP/Wide World, p. 105; Courtesy of the Bancroft Library, University of California, Berkeley, p. 33; Library of Congress, pp. 3, 11, 17, 28, 36, 42, 46, 50, 59, 75, 90, 99, 108, 110; Lloyd Degrane, p. 97; Photographs and Prints Division, Schomburg Center for Research in Black Culture, The New York Public Library, Astor, Lenox and Tilden Foundations, pp. 4, 56, 65, 81; Vivian G. Harsh Research Collection of Afro-American History and Literature, Chicago Public Library, pp. 48, 85.

Cover Illustrations: Library of Congress.

Contents

Chapter 1

The Pulitzer Prize

I f there was no electricity in the house, they might as well go to the movies. That is what Gwendolyn Brooks was thinking on May 1, 1950.[1] As day turned to evening, she and her son were finding it hard to see in their two-room Chicago apartment. Her husband, Henry Blakely, was trying to get the electricity restored. Their constant money problems had made the family late paying the bill. As a result, the electric company had turned off their service.

Blakely had recently started his own business repairing automobiles, and he was still struggling to make a success of it. The thirty-two-year-old Brooks earned a small and irregular income from writing. Harper and Brothers Publishing had paid her only $100 before publishing her latest book of poetry, *Annie Allen*. She expected to make more money as copies of the book were sold, but that would take time. The publisher feared that *Annie Allen* would not sell as well as her first book had.

As Brooks and her eight-year-old son, Henry, slipped on their coats, the telephone rang. A reporter for the *Chicago Sun-Times* was on the line. "Did you know you have won the Pulitzer Prize?" he asked. Brooks screamed with surprise and joy. "I couldn't believe it," she said later. "My son and I danced around in the dusk."[2]

Young Henry could not believe it either. "You didn't. Didn't. Didn't," he insisted. Brooks called her mother with the news. "You didn't," Keziah Brooks stammered. Brooks then called her husband. "You didn't," Blakely exclaimed. She called several friends, and all had the same reaction.[3]

By then, darkness had engulfed the apartment. Brooks and her son hurried off belatedly to the movies. As they traveled to the theater, she observed the people passing by. None of them knew who she was, Brooks thought. None of them were aware that she had just won the 1950 Pulitzer Prize in poetry for *Annie Allen*, the book her publisher expected to sell so poorly.[4] She sat through the film in a daze.

The next day Brooks sent a telegraph to her editor. "Am sick with happiness and know how glad you are for me," she told Elizabeth

"Nobody believed it. Not even my little boy believed it. . . . And I guess I didn't believe it either—at first."[5]

The Pulitzer Prize

Joseph Pulitzer (1847–1911) owned a number of newspapers, including the *St. Louis Post-Dispatch* and the *New York World*. When he died, Pulitzer left $2 million to start a school of journalism at Columbia University in New York City. He also wanted the school to give annual awards for excellence in journalism and the arts. The first Pulitzer Prizes were awarded in 1917.

Lawrence.[6] At the same time, congratulatory telegrams poured into the Brooks home. The telephone rang off the hook with calls from old friends and requests for interviews. A stream of reporters and photographers traipsed through the apartment.

Those who came during the day caused Brooks no worry, but as twilight fell she began to fret. Reporters from Chicago's premier newspaper, the *Tribune*, had not arrived yet. Her electricity was still off. What if the interviewer needed it? Sure enough, when the *Tribune* staffers showed up, the photographer looked around for an electrical outlet. "I sat there frozen," Brooks said later. She waited in fear as he plugged in his lighting equipment. Miraculously, the light shone. Henry Blakely had come through. "So that's the story of the Pulitzer Prize," she said. "Light in darkness."[7]

The attention continued nonstop. Curious people kept dropping by the apartment to see what Brooks looked like. Most of them were from her neighborhood. "There was no telling *how* I impressed them," Brooks said.[8] Two of the visitors, however, were white women from one of the city's exclusive neighborhoods, who would normally not have ventured into Chicago's all-black South Side. Brooks felt they treated her rather snootily. She later got her revenge by portraying them satirically in a poem, "The Lovers of the Poor."[9]

Several callers asked Brooks for advice about breaking into writing. Others wanted her to critique their poetry. One person even presented her with eighty poems. Brooks tactfully declined, calling herself an inadequate critic. She did, however, take the opportunity to sell several of the would-be poets copies of her book.

Requests poured in for Brooks to do poetry readings or give lectures on race relations. The shy and quiet author refused most of these. At this early stage in her career, public speaking made her nervous. She strongly preferred writing as her platform. "When you make a mistake on paper you can correct it, but you have to live with a mistake when you express it while speaking," she said.[10]

Despite all the attention, Brooks told a reporter that she felt unchanged after winning the prize. Her husband assured another reporter, "Gwen is the most sincere person I've ever known."[11] But her son wanted things to go back to the way they were. Too many people were asking him questions. "I don't like to be so famous," he said. "You have too many people talking to you. You never have any peace."[12]

❖ ❖ ❖

The Pulitzer Prizes were administered by Columbia University's school of journalism. In New York City, a reporter for the *Amsterdam News*, an African-American newspaper, phoned Columbia with a question: Was Brooks the first person of her race to win a Pulitzer? A spokesman for the university replied that the judges had not been aware of Brooks's skin color. They did not see a photograph of her until after the award was made. In any case, he added, the university kept no records of the winners' races and could not say.[13] The answer to the reporter's question was actually a simple yes.

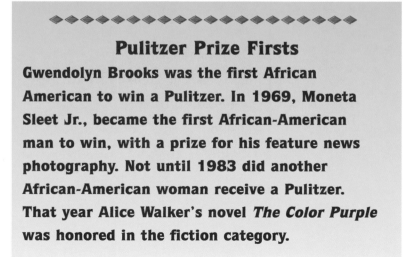

Pulitzer Prize Firsts

Gwendolyn Brooks was the first African American to win a Pulitzer. In 1969, Moneta Sleet Jr., became the first African-American man to win, with a prize for his feature news photography. Not until 1983 did another African-American woman receive a Pulitzer. That year Alice Walker's novel *The Color Purple* was honored in the fiction category.

Chapter 2

A Sparkly Childhood

I can't understand why my mother had to go back to Kansas," Gwendolyn Brooks once said with a laugh, claiming that her mother had "ruined" her birth. Instead of staying in Chicago with her husband, the pregnant Mrs. Brooks had returned to her parents' home in Topeka, Kansas. As a result, Gwendolyn Elizabeth was born on June 7, 1917, in Kansas, rather than in her beloved hometown. "If I had known that she was going to become so famous," Mrs. Brooks retorted, "I would have made certain that she was born in Chicago."[1]

Baby Gwendolyn soon moved into her parents' apartment in the Hyde Park neighborhood of Chicago. Her doting mother never allowed her to crawl. Instead, as soon as Gwendolyn could stand, family members led her by the hand from place to place. When Gwendolyn was sixteen months old, her brother, Raymond, was born.

Topeka, Kansas, above, is where Brooks was born,
though she always considered her hometown to be Chicago.

Mrs. Brooks was the former Keziah Corine Wims of
Topeka, one of ten children. As teenagers, most of the
brothers and sisters went to work, but Keziah and her
older sister Beulah thirsted for more education. Beulah
graduated from a local teacher's college. After she started
teaching, she gave Keziah money to help pay for college.
Keziah also worked as a maid to make ends meet. She
studied piano as well as teaching others to play. Secretly
she yearned to become a concert pianist, a dream she did

not fulfill. Still, singing, playing, and composing music became her lifelong pleasure. Eventually, she earned a teaching certificate and took a job teaching fifth grade in Topeka. During the summer of 1914, while visiting one of her sisters in Chicago, Keziah met David Anderson Brooks and fell in love.

David Brooks's passion for education was as strong as his future wife's. His personal quest to educate himself had been even more dramatic. Though he was born in Kansas, David's family moved to the Oklahoma Territory to homestead when he was nine years old. There, the family of fourteen braved persecution by some of the other homesteaders, who were racists. They hated all African Americans for no reason other than the color of their skin.

The Brookses' horses and mules were poisoned. The family was run off its land at gunpoint. They were reduced to living in a tent-covered dugout shack. One of David's sisters died, then a second. Finally, David's father was stricken with pneumonia. This stern but forceful man had escaped from slavery and become a Union soldier during the Civil War. On his deathbed, he called his sons to him and instructed each to take a single stick and break it. They easily did so. Then he told each to find a second stick and tie them all together. No matter how hard they tried, the sons could not break the sticks once they were bound and united. "Family ties," said their father, meaning they would be stronger as a group than each man alone.[2]

Though not the eldest son, David became the head of the family. He was a young teenager but worked like a full-grown man. Sometimes the desire to go fishing or play ball like other boys became so great that he would put his little brothers and sisters to bed early. Hoping they would fall instantly to sleep so he could play, he closed their eyes for them. "As if they wouldn't open them right back up," he said later.[3]

> Gwendolyn's parents shared a deep passion for education.

David was determined to finish high school, even though he had to rise at 5 A.M. to feed his employer's horses. At graduation, his teachers gave him the honor of performing both a speech and a song. Then his employer, the mayor of Oklahoma City, presented him with a bouquet of roses.

David dreamed of becoming a doctor, but he did not have the money to go directly to college. After several more years of scrimping and saving, he enrolled at Fisk University in Nashville, Tennessee. Sadly, his savings ran out after little more than a year. Like many other African Americans, David became part of the Great Migration to the North. He moved to Chicago, hoping to continue his education part-time, but this was not to be. Still, he never gave up his interest in medicine. After he married Keziah and became a father, he nursed Gwendolyn and Raymond tenderly through their childhood illnesses. Often, he

◆◆◆◆◆◆◆◆◆◆

The Great Migration

In 1910, ninety percent of African Americans still lived in the South. The outbreak of World War I in 1914 led to the Great Migration, an exodus of African Americans to the cities of the North. By 1920, as many as a million southerners had moved in search of better jobs and greater freedom. Blacks filled jobs vacated by white soldiers, as well as new jobs created by the war effort. Despite job and housing discrimination, these African Americans often felt free for the first time. Education was better, and they could vote, a right that was often denied to them in the South.

dosed them with medicines he brewed himself using recipes from books and from the folk traditions he had grown up with.

Though the dreams of both David and Keziah had been dashed, neither became bitter. They resolved instead to provide their children, Gwendolyn and Raymond, with a happy, secure, and safe childhood. Above all, they determined that their children would be well educated at home and at school.

Even before his marriage, David Brooks had put aside money to buy a set of the *Harvard Classics*, the greatest books of the European literary tradition. He viewed it as an investment in the children he hoped to have. For a wedding present, he gave his wife a beautiful glass-fronted bookcase to hold these treasures. When they became parents,

David and Keziah Brooks read aloud to their children from this home library.

"Our parents were intelligent and courageous; they subscribed to duty, decency, dignity, industry," said their daughter, Gwendolyn, years later.[4] They did not "put on airs. I hate that with a passion—people who think they are too good for their own folk," she said.[5]

By the time Gwendolyn was four years old, her parents had saved enough money to buy their own home. The two-story gray house sat on a secluded street of Chicago's South Side. Keziah Brooks planted hedges, shrubs, trees, and flowers. The children could play on the front and back porches, as well as in a backyard sandbox. They joined playmates from the neighborhood in games of tag and hide-and-seek, or in lazy conversations on the hot summer evenings.

Gwendolyn loved sitting on the back porch, which faced the sunset in the west. In the evening she watched the changing patterns of "red streaks" and "gold worlds," she said later.[6] During the day she watched the clouds scudding past, making pictures in the sky. Sometimes she imagined that she saw the future there. In actuality, the porch faced the backs of a row of run-down tenement apartments, but Gwendolyn never noticed them. She was always looking up—at the sky.

> David and Keziah Brooks put all their hopes into giving their children a good start in life.

> "I was at my happiest, sitting out on the back porch, to sit there and look out at the western sky with all those beautiful changing clouds and just to dream about the future."[7]

David Brooks worked as a janitor and shipping clerk for the McKinley Music Company in downtown Chicago. Though a longtime employee, his salary was meager. He often painted houses on the side. As an additional source of income, the Brookses rented the second floor of their house to another family. Keziah Brooks, like most wives of that period, was a full-time mother and homemaker.

Gwendolyn's parents often sacrificed their own needs to give their children the best. Every Easter, she and her brother were outfitted in new clothes from head to toe. Their mother bought no more than a new hat for herself, while their father wore his old clothes.

Mrs. Brooks took Gwendolyn and Raymond to church at the Carter Temple Colored Methodist Episcopal Church. It was down the block from their home. When Gwendolyn was as young as four or five, her mother coached her in memorizing and reciting poetry at church programs. Mr. Brooks was not a church-goer. "His religion was kindness," his daughter said.[8]

Her childhood was nothing less than "sparkly," the poet said later.[9] The Brooks family particularly enjoyed

**Brooks grew up on the South Side of Chicago,
an African-American area of the city.**

celebrating holidays together. Their table always groaned under a spread of delicious dishes for every occasion. Gwendolyn feasted on turkey, fruitcake, and angel-food cake at Christmas; mince, apple, and pumpkin pies at Thanksgiving; ham and chocolate rabbits at Easter; devil's-food and coconut cakes when visiting relatives; ice cream molded into fruit and flower shapes for birthdays.

Gwendolyn's mother was one of four sisters, so there were lots of aunts and uncles who adored Gwendolyn and

> Lots of aunts and uncles lavished their love on young Gwendolyn and her brother, adding to the contentment of their early years.

Raymond. Aunt Eppie and her husband were raising three adopted children on a fourteen-acre farm near Kalamazoo, Michigan. Aunt Ella was the poorest of her mother's sisters, though there was always laughter in her house when Gwendolyn's father played cards and argued politics with Uncle Ernest.

Aunt Beulah, who had lent her sister Keziah money for college, was the "Queen" of the family.[10] Beulah Wims was single and had a successful career teaching cooking and sewing at the segregated black high school in Tulsa, Oklahoma. She was an expert seamstress and made all Gwendolyn's clothes for many years. Gwendolyn especially treasured a stylish pair of beach pajamas her aunt had sewn. Aunt Beulah took summer courses at the University of Chicago and lavished presents and attention on her niece and nephew whenever she was in town.

Gwendolyn's favorite aunt was Gertrude, despite the always terrifying journey to her house in the suburb of Lilydale. The reason for Gwendolyn's terror was the infestation of grasshoppers in the fields around the home. The Brooks family would ride the streetcar from the South Side of the city. On arriving, Gwendolyn would race to her aunt's front door. She kept her eyes closed, and her fingers in her ears, until she arrived safely inside.

Gertrude's husband, a former jazz pianist, had a good job with the city of Chicago. The house in Lilydale was new and beautifully furnished. It even had an electric refrigerator, rather than an icebox, which seemed like the height of luxury to Gwendolyn. At Aunt Gertrude's house, Gwendolyn was treated like a princess. Her brother, Raymond, correctly observed, "You just like to go out there because they think you're pretty." To Gwendolyn, this was fair, because she considered Raymond the favorite in their own home.[11]

Not until she entered first grade at the nearby Forestville Elementary School did any unhappiness mark Gwendolyn's young life. On her block, she felt comfortable with the children she knew. But at heart she was a shy, solitary child who did not make new friends easily. In school, her delight in learning to read, listening to stories, and painting pictures was marred by the teasing of the other African-American first-graders. They called her "Ol' Black Gal."[12]

This puzzled Gwendolyn. She had always considered her skin color "beautiful." Examining her arm, she had decided its chocolate brown was "charming."[13] Yet her lighter-skinned classmates taunted her. Even more

> In school, learning to read opened up a new world for Gwendolyn.

confusing, classmates with skin like hers or darker also called her a name—"stuck up."[14] In response, Gwendolyn withdrew from the other children. She took solace in reading and began devouring a book or more a day. Almost as soon as she became a reader, she became a writer.

Chapter 3

"You Have Talent"

 ne day, Keziah Brooks found her seven-year-old daughter in a small red chair in her room after school. Gwendolyn bent intently over the paper on which she wrote. Mrs. Brooks asked to see her daughter's work, finding seven or eight rhymes of two lines each. The startled but delighted Mrs. Brooks exclaimed that Gwendolyn would be "as great as Paul Laurence Dunbar."[1] Dunbar, the most popular African-American poet of the period, was a great favorite of David Brooks. He owned Dunbar's collected works and often recited the poems to his children from memory. "[My mother] said I was going to be a poet!" Gwendolyn said later. "What can you do when your mama tells you that?"[2]

Mrs. Brooks decided to give her daughter as much time to write as she wished. Gwendolyn had only one

> "My mother decided that I was to be the female Paul Laurence Dunbar. I believed every word she said."[3]

chore throughout most of her childhood: washing the dinner dishes. During her free time, the girl shut herself in her room to read and write. She always ate dinner with a book propped open before her, unless the family had company. Sometimes, worrying that Gwendolyn needed to rest her eyes and brain, Mrs. Brooks forced her daughter to go outside and play.

Soon the girl felt that writing had become necessary to her existence, "like breathing or eating," she said later, "something almost holy."[4] She wrote happily, without regard for what others might think. Sometimes though, she buried sheaves of poems in her yard. She pretended that years in the future someone might dig them up, read them, and marvel at the forgotten writer's talent.

One day, a building on the Brookses' street caught fire and grew into a mighty blaze. As all the neighbors ran to see it, Mrs. Brooks opened her daughter's door. She urged Gwendolyn to come see the awesome sight. Gwendolyn did not even look up from her writing. Absent-mindedly, she murmured some phrase of agreement. Mrs. Brooks quietly closed the door again, leaving her daughter to her work.

The parents' faith in their odd, intense child paid off. When Gwendolyn was eleven years old, four of her poems were published in a local newspaper, the *Hyde Parker*. At thirteen, she had her first publication in a national magazine, *American Childhood*. For this poem, "Eventide," her payment was six copies of the October 1930 issue it appeared in.

That same year, however, the Great Depression brought the Brooks family finances to the crisis point. Though Mr. Brooks had kept his job, his salary was cut once, then a second time. The family ate beans for dinner day after day. Mrs. Brooks, desperate to make ends meet, urged her husband to find a new and better-paying job. He refused to give up his secure but poorly-paid position for the uncertainty of the job market.

When school let out for the summer, Mrs. Brooks took Gwendolyn and Raymond to Kansas. After they had been with the Wims family for several months, Mr. Brooks arrived and asked for his children. He took them back with him to Chicago, leaving his wife behind. For a year, he cared for them as a single parent. Finally, Mrs. Brooks

The Great Depression

After the stock market crash of 1929, the United States went into the worst economic slump in its history. Thousands of banks and businesses failed, and millions of people lost their jobs. By the early 1930s, 15 percent of American workers were unemployed, and the number was growing. African-American workers suffered even more. In cities like Chicago and New York, up to half of African-American households had no breadwinners.

rejoined her husband. Although she had missed her mother keenly, Gwendolyn lashed out at her for abandoning them.[5]

Her family had reunited, but Gwendolyn's world would never again be as secure. As the Great Depression worsened, she was about to enter high school and a painful adolescence. Years later she reminisced without fondness about her teen years. "Today I find people who'll come up to me and say, 'Gwen! Remember the good times we used to have in school?' And I remember those days too well." Throughout her adolescence, Gwendolyn felt different, unwanted, like an outsider, yet powerless to change herself. She rarely reached out to make friends and joined no clubs or organizations.[6]

In upper elementary school, Gwendolyn had attended a few parties and dances with disastrous results. Only the light-skinned daughters of the neighborhood's African-American elite, doctors, lawyers, and teachers, got asked to dance. Then the young teenagers began to play kissing games. The same few girls sneaked out into the hallway to rendezvous with the boys who had won their kisses. "I was timid to the point of terror, silent, primly dressed," she said later. "AND DARK."[7]

Once again, Gwendolyn withdrew into reading and writing. Once again, she blossomed as a writer.

During her childhood, Gwendolyn had regularly visited the Forestville Branch of the Chicago Public Library, which she later dubbed "Enchantment-land."[8] As a teen, she discovered on the shelves one of the first anthologies of African-American poetry, *Caroling Dusk*. Edited by the poet Countee Cullen, it featured his work as well as that of his friend Langston Hughes. For Gwendolyn, it was a revelation to learn how many other African Americans wrote poetry.

One poem particularly excited her: Hughes's "The Weary Blues." It showed her how important it might be to write about ordinary African Americans. And it gave her hope. "If these people could write poetry and become well known," she thought, "maybe I would also become well known one day."[9]

The Harlem Renaissance

An explosion of African-American talent in literature, fine arts, music, and theater took New York City by storm in the 1920s. Countee Cullen, James Weldon Johnson, and Langston Hughes were among the outstanding writers in the movement known as the Harlem Renaissance.

More than twenty novels, poetry collections, memoirs, and other books saw publication before the renaissance was brought to an end by the Great Depression in the mid-thirties. Among the authors were Arna Bontemps, Dorothy West, and Zora Neale Hurston. African-American writers would not be published in such great numbers again until the 1960s.

She also discovered the magazine *Writer's Digest*. This journal taught her the practical side of writing for a living. It listed book and magazine publishers, itemizing which ones published poetry and how much they paid. She realized that plenty of other writers waited with pounding hearts for the mail to come with news of whether their work had been accepted or rejected.[10]

Gwendolyn began to submit poems to "Lights and Shadows," the new poetry column of the *Chicago Defender* newspaper. This weekly African-American-owned paper covered local and national events and was distributed nationwide. Soon she became a regular contributor, her poems appearing week after week. Seventy-five of them would eventually win publication in the *Chicago Defender* during her high school and junior college years. The proud author created her own book of them, pasting the clippings into a hardbound journal.

The teenaged Gwendolyn stirred up trouble when she founded her own local newspaper, the *Champlain Weekly News*. Mrs. Brooks, though not a gossip herself, often lent her friends a sympathetic ear. By "accidentally" overhearing these confidences and by eavesdropping on the conversations of her family's second-floor tenants, Gwendolyn found enough news to fill her paper. For a few weeks, five cents bought a handwritten account of everybody's

> Plenty of other writers also waited, hearts pounding, for news from the publishers.

business. "[People were] greatly relieved when I gave up my career as newspaperwoman," she said later.[11]

Hour after hour, Gwendolyn sat in her room, writing at the beautiful, old-fashioned desk given to her by her father. She loved its many small compartments and long, narrow drawers. She arrayed her most cherished books in its glass-fronted top shelf. Among them were the "Emily" books, about a Canadian girl much like herself. Emily dreamed, kept notebooks, and yearned to be a writer. Gwendolyn so wished she might meet the books' author, L. M. Montgomery, who had also written *Anne of Green Gables*. "But who ever met an Author?" she thought.[12]

When Gwendolyn sent a selection of her poems to the writer James Weldon Johnson, he surprised her with a cordial reply. Johnson was renowned for composing "Lift Ev'ry Voice and Sing," known as the "Negro National Anthem." At this time, he also served as the secretary of the National Association for the Advancement of Colored People (NAACP). Johnson wrote that he considered her an "unquestionable talent."[13] He also urged her to study modern poets. This was good advice for a girl who, though steeped in the traditional British and American poets, had read little twentieth-century poetry.

Not much later, Mrs. Brooks heard that Johnson

> Gwendolyn filled a notebook with newspaper clippings of her poems.

Sixteen-year-old Gwendolyn was excited but shy
about meeting the writer James Weldon Johnson.

would give a lecture at a nearby church. She and her daughter excitedly attended. Mrs. Brooks prodded Gwendolyn to join the line of admirers waiting to speak to Johnson after his talk. When the girl's turn came, she timidly and silently shook his hand. Mrs. Brooks could not contain herself. "She's the one who sent you the poems!" she blurted. Gwendolyn would not forget the tall, handsome, and erect Johnson drawing himself up, crossing his hands in front of him, and wearily answering, "I get so many of them, you know." Sixty years later, having met her own share of aspiring teenage poets, Brooks realized that his response had been "perfectly reasonable." Nevertheless, she said, it had left the Brookses a bit "chilled."[14]

What a contrast it was when mother and daughter met Langston Hughes at another church event soon afterward. Mrs. Brooks armed herself with a sheaf of Gwendolyn's poems. An usher tried to keep them from approaching Hughes after his talk. Mrs. Brooks barged past him. "My daughter *writes*," she announced.[15]

Hughes "was entirely different," according to Gwendolyn Brooks. He sat down and read her poems. "'You're talented,' he told her. 'Keep writing. Some day you'll have a book published.'" Sixty years later, Brooks would smile at the memory: "That did mean a lot to a sixteen-year-old girl."[16]

As a teenager, Gwendolyn clashed regularly with her forceful, strong-willed mother. Like most parents of the day, Mrs. Brooks still sometimes disciplined her adolescent children with an open hand or a light switch cut from a backyard tree. One day, she gave Gwendolyn a spanking. The young woman received it without moving, without speaking, without crying. The surprised and frustrated Mrs. Brooks demanded that her husband repeat the punishment when he got home from work. Again, Gwendolyn stood silent and unmoving, but this time, Mrs. Brooks burst into tears herself.[17]

Underneath her reserved exterior, Gwendolyn wrestled with the mood swings and strong emotions of adolescence. She agonized through a series of crushes on boys who often did not know she existed. She poured her feelings into dozens of very bad poems on love, usually on love's suffering and pain. She imagined being married to the boy of her dreams, loved passionately by him.[18]

High school would prove to be a struggle.

Chapter 4

Daughter of the Dusk

For three years, Gwendolyn transferred from one high school to another, searching for a good fit. She spent her freshman year at the nearly all-white Hyde Park Branch High School. Her first daily venture outside Chicago's black community came as a shock. Black students were not mistreated there; they were completely ignored. "None of [the whites] would have anything to do with you," she said.[1]

Her next-door neighbor then recommended all-black Wendell Phillips High School. Gwendolyn would "have a ball" there, her neighbor predicted. But her sophomore year at Phillips proved just as painful as the previous one had been. Phillips students were far more "hip" than she, Brooks said later. She slunk anonymously from class to class, hoping not to be noticed. She made "two friends, if that."[2]

Finally, as a junior, she settled on the racially mixed Englewood High School. Gwendolyn had not been invited to any parties at the other two high schools. When she made some friends at Englewood, she decided to throw a party of her own. Her mother and three aunts pitched in to decorate the house and prepare refreshments. Gwendolyn spent most of the evening sitting, hands folded, frozen with embarrassment when only a few classmates arrived.

"I just slumped through the halls, real quiet, hugging my books."[3]

Gwendolyn's New Year's resolutions for 1934, her senior year, show what a serious and different girl she was. Gwendolyn resolved to write poetry and prose every day and to get her pieces published. But she also urged herself to draw, sing, practice piano, and improvise musically. Most uniquely, she promised to "invent several dances, including variations on the tap dance." Personally, she hoped to become "softer-mannered" and "pleasanter."[4]

It was at Englewood that a teacher first encouraged her to write. A very strict history teacher assigned her class to write a report on a historical novel called *Janice Meredith*. The book left Gwendolyn so bored she barely finished it. To amuse herself, she decided to write the paper in humorous rhyme. The astonished teacher gave her an A. Intrigued at her student's originality, she encouraged Gwendolyn to write more.

When she was a senior, Gwendolyn enrolled in a

journalism class. As a result, she felt comfortable enough to join her first school club, the newspaper. She submitted poems to the paper, which were published. One piece caught the whole school's attention. It was a rhymed story about a high school girl who signs up for all the courses taken by the boy on whom she has a crush. But the courses are so hard that she flunks out and loses him forever.

The journalism teacher focused on Gwendolyn. She took time to ask about her background, her aspirations, how she got her ideas. One day, teacher and student met by chance on the streetcar. As they chatted, the teacher shared her enthusiasm for Gwendolyn's writing. She urged her to keep it up after graduation. Though embarrassed to have been overheard by strangers on the streetcar, Gwendolyn glowed.

When she graduated in 1934, the United States lay deep in economic depression. Half of

Teenaged Gwendolyn was already a published poet.

◆ ◆ ◆ ◆ ◆

Chicago's African Americans were unemployed. Mr. Brooks now permanently worked two jobs. Gwendolyn's brother, also a high school student, had a part-time job. As a result, Mrs. Brooks shouldered many of her husband and son's household responsibilities. This left Gwendolyn no choice but to do more housework herself.

The young woman's future was very uncertain because the family could not afford to send her to college. Scholarships and loans like the ones now available were rare in those days. Still, Gwendolyn could not have been happier to put high school behind her. "What ecstasy it is to graduate," she wrote.[5]

It was Gwendolyn's good fortune that the city of Chicago founded a public two-year college just as she finished high school. Woodrow Wilson Junior College was supported by funds from President Franklin Roosevelt's New Deal, which was intended to help people during the Great Depression. Wilson charged just $6 tuition for each semester. Even this small sum constituted a week's wages for many people during those hard times.

> In 1934, half of the African Americans in Chicago were unemployed.

Gwendolyn registered for courses in Latin and English, intending to major in languages. "I knew that I was going to be a writer," she said.[6] She began to haunt the college library, discovering the works of new poets, including Emily Dickinson. She experimented with writing poetry portraits of people she knew, such as classmates, teachers, and members of her family. She also wrote word pictures of people in the news, like the new African-American boxing champion Joe Louis. Again Gwendolyn wrote to James Weldon Johnson. He critiqued her work carefully, writing many comments on her poems. He criticized one word choice as "atrocious."[7] But he also accepted one poem for publication in the NAACP magazine *The Crisis*.

◆◆◆◆◆◆◆◆◆

The New Deal

In 1933, President Franklin Roosevelt's New Deal program was launched to help the United States bounce back from the Great Depression. Agencies were set up to help needy people, to create jobs for the unemployed, and to encourage business recovery and growth.

Some of Gwendolyn's friends from Englewood also attended Wilson, giving her a ready-made social circle. She began dating for the first time. Young men had no money to spend on dinners or movies during the Depression, but Gwendolyn enjoyed taking walks with her dates or talking to them in her family's living room. The two years of junior college ended all too quickly.

Gwendolyn needed a job after graduation in 1936. The editor of the "Lights and Shadows" column suggested she apply to be a reporter for the *Chicago Defender*, which had been publishing her poems for years. Gwendolyn arrived at the interview accompanied by her mother.

This picture of the Chicago business district was taken in 1934, the year Brooks started studying at Chicago's Woodrow Wilson Junior College.

Publisher Robert S. Abbott had expected to interview a possible reporter—not a reporter and her mom. His facial expression made it immediately clear she would not be hired, Brooks realized. In later years, though, she was glad that journalism had not sidetracked her from her dedication to poetry.[8]

For a while Brooks alternated unemployment with work as a maid in wealthy Chicago homes. Finally, she took a position as a "typist," beginning what she called "the most horrible four months of my existence."[9] True, *some* typing was required by Dr. E. N. French, her new employer. This West Indian "spiritual adviser," who wore a little black skullcap to work, had his four secretaries type lists of random numbers, clip them, and mail them to clients who paid him for lucky numbers. He also had his employees mix up bottles of colored water, which he sold as love potions.

The secretaries even made home deliveries of these bottled charms to customers who lived in the Mecca Building, where Dr. French's office was located. The Mecca had once been a grand Chicago apartment building. Its landlords were now squeezing hundreds of poor African Americans into one-room tenements carved from the large old apartments. As Gwendolyn trudged up and down the stairs making deliveries, she saw "loves, lonelinesses, hates, jealousies . . . charity, sainthood, glory, shame, despair, fear."[10] Years later, she would revisit this experience with a poetry collection, *In the Mecca*.

Though she hated the job and French's deception, Gwendolyn did not feel she could quit. Dr. French paid $8 a week, a good salary for a typist, and her parents needed the $2 weekly that she gave them. Then Dr. French announced that since Gwendolyn spoke well, she would become his assistant pastor at the storefront church he ran on the side. She would even preach at the upcoming Sunday service. This was too much, and Gwendolyn refused, losing her job. Eventually, she took a series of other typing positions, mostly in lawyers' offices.

During this low point in her life, Gwendolyn joined the NAACP Youth Council, a group of men and women in their twenties. The Youth Council debated current racial issues and publicly demonstrated against racism and injustice. At one demonstration, the young people protested the shameful crime of lynching by marching with symbolic chains around their necks.

Gwendolyn made friends there and for the first time felt really accepted by people of her own age.[11] Like Gwendolyn, many of them were writers or artists. They included Margaret Taylor, who later founded Chicago's DuSable Museum, and John Johnson, whose Johnson Publishing Co. would produce *Ebony* and *Jet* magazines. She now had "a whole bunch of friends, of people who seemed to like me and thought that there was something to me," she said.[12]

The NAACP Youth Council also held parties, dances, and other meetings. At one event, Gwendolyn looked up to see "this glorious man [who] appeared in the doorway and posed for a moment, looking the situation over." Gwendolyn looked back at him. "I was always impressed by dignity in a man, and he certainly had that," she said later. Boldly, she said to her friend Margaret Taylor, "There is the man I'm going to marry."

Not skipping a beat, Margaret hollered, "Hey, boy, this girl wants to meet you."[13]

Chapter 5

Wife, Mother, Poet

Henry Lowington Blakely Jr. remembered it this way: He had been dating a young woman named Sarah on and off for several years. One night, they went on a church-group hayride. Everyone paired off for some cuddling and kissing. He and Sarah did too. After a while, it was all too clear that nothing was clicking between them. But Sarah had an idea. "I know just the girl for you," she said.[1]

She told Blakely that this person would be at the next meeting of the Youth Council. He made sure to go. As he found his seat, he heard Margaret Taylor call to him. Just then the young woman in question, Miss Brooks, got up to give a report. Blakely studied her. He noticed her "slim, brown frame" and her voice "rich and deep." He said he "sensed through that voice that almost all of her shining was inward, and I felt warm in that shining."[2]

Brooks and Blakely hit it off immediately. They both read avidly. They also both loved the movies and stepping out for parties and social events. They found they could talk to each other endlessly on any topic. Blakely grew to love David and Keziah Brooks, and they loved him. Years later, Keziah Brooks continued to admire him for his willingness to take her daughter on "dates," even after many years of marriage. She supported his courtliness by always offering to babysit for their children.

Henry Blakely Jr. was a native Chicagoan. His father had left his mother for another woman when Henry was thirteen. Henry Sr., a steamfitter and successful contractor, spent much time and money tinkering with inventions. Henry Sr.'s wife had grown so frustrated with the expense of these projects that she smashed one to bits.

Henry Sr. stayed in his three sons' lives, but saw them rarely after he had a second family. Gwendolyn Brooks always believed Henry Jr. never got over this experience. When Blakely later published his first book of poetry in 1974, its signature poem addressed this loving but complex relationship with his father.

Blakely had graduated from a vocational high school, where he developed a mechanical talent like his father's. But he yearned for more. At the time he met his future wife, Blakely was attending Wilson Junior College. He also sold insurance part-time, having just received his agent's license. Like Brooks, he had been writing poetry since childhood. He had come to the NAACP Youth Council meeting hoping to find a soulmate in Brooks, and he did.

Pearl Blakely did not want her son to begin a serious relationship. Like many single mothers of sons, she had fiercely disciplined and guarded her boys from the dangers of inner-city life. She believed Henry was too dreamy to marry.[3] Still a student, he had never supported himself, much less a wife and family.

Nevertheless, he proposed to Brooks. When the wedding invitations were mailed, an outraged Pearl Blakely confronted Gwendolyn and Keziah Brooks. She demanded that the marriage not take place. Her son was as immature as a teenager, she said.[4] He was so poor that he did not even have a suit to wear to the wedding. The Brookses considered her words, but Gwendolyn decided to marry him anyway.

The wedding was celebrated on September 17, 1939, a Sunday afternoon, in the Brookses' living room. Gwendolyn wore a red velvet dress that had cost nearly a week's salary. Henry wore a brand-new grayish-blue suit, a wedding present from his favorite aunt. A friend sang the hymn "O Promise Me." When the preacher asked who gave the bride in marriage, there was silence for a moment. Though her husband stood next to her, Keziah Brooks answered, "I do."[5] Henry Blakely's wedding gift to his wife was a love poem.

The young couple could not afford a honeymoon. They went straight to their one-room kitchenette apartment. Though Brooks said she felt "bleak" when she saw how small and worn it was, the newlyweds enjoyed their new companionship.[6] They sometimes stayed up all night reading and wrote together side by side.

Unfortunately, their money problems began almost immediately. Blakely switched to selling life insurance full-time for an African-American company. He found,

Once-elegant apartment buildings were hacked into one- and two-room "kitchenettes" that were rented to African Americans.

however, that his poor clients often skipped their insurance payments when a more pressing bill came due. To compensate, the company would then reduce Blakely's pay.

Like her mother, Brooks kept house, but not full-time. Both she and her husband viewed writing as her work. Pearl Blakely, who already irritated her daughter-in-law with criticism of her housework, soon grew exasperated with the young couple. "Poetry ain't going to make you no living," she insisted.[7] In fact, Henry Blakely wrote less and less as the years went on. As his wife became more successful, he assumed the role of her first and favorite critic and editor. All her life, Brooks gave her husband credit for being the most supportive partner a woman writer could ever have.

None of this, unfortunately, paid the rent. Housing was extremely hard to find in 1940. Tens of thousands of unemployed people had moved to Chicago in search of work during the Depression. Housing discrimination against African Americans was practiced openly at this time. Neighborhoods were identified as black or white, and the black neighborhoods were full to bursting.

Even their dreary honeymoon kitchenette soon became too expensive. First the couple moved to a furnished room in someone else's home. Then they found another apartment at a low cost, since the one bathroom at the end of the hall was shared by five families. Several years later, Brooks would write a poem called "Kitchenette

Building." The characters in the poem are so worn down that they would rather snatch time alone in a communal bathtub, whose water never got hotter than lukewarm, than dream of greater things.

The Blakelys' son, Henry III, was born on October 10, 1940. Brooks went into labor as she walked down the hall from the shared bathroom. Her labor progressed so quickly that she could not get to the hospital. She gave birth in her own bed. A local doctor arrived only in time to cut the umbilical cord and announce that the baby was a boy.

African-American Literature in the 1930s and 1940s

Relatively few books by African-American authors were published during these years. Langston Hughes was still the leading poet and also wrote articles, a memoir, and fiction. For African Americans, perhaps the best-loved poem of these decades was "For My People" by Margaret Walker. Other poets of the time included Sterling Brown, Melvin B. Tolson, and Robert Hayden. Highlights of fiction included Zora Neale Hurston's masterpiece *Their Eyes Were Watching God* (1937) and Richard Wright's *Native Son* (1940), which became the first best-seller by an African-American author. Wright's autobiography *Black Boy* came out to both praise and controversy in 1945.

Both parents greeted Henry's birth joyfully, despite their slim finances. Still, Brooks admitted having been "a nervous wreck. . . . I didn't understand anything about children and he was an experiment."[8] For the next year, she willingly gave up writing. "I gave a lot of attention to my children," she said years later. "I do not regret doing that."[9]

The family moved again a few months after Henry's birth to a converted garage apartment. When the baby developed pneumonia in the damp rooms, Blakely suggested they share an apartment with his brother. Brooks refused, demanding an apartment with privacy. Tension between them exploded when an argument on the Fourth of July led Blakely to flip a firecracker in Brooks's direction. She took the baby and went home to her parents, saying the marriage was over. Her father intervened and persuaded them to try again. "Gwendolyn wants something she'll never find," he confided to his wife. "Perfect happiness."[10]

The year 1941 was more stable. Blakely found a job in a defense plant, making supplies for the military. The United States had just entered World War II. As an older, married man, Blakely was not called to fight, but he did join the National Guard. The family moved to a second-floor apartment above a real-estate office, where they were to remain for seven years. When they first turned on the radiators, legions of mice came streaming out. Brooks leaped onto a chair, screaming. Blakely mischievously chanted, "HUP two three four" to the marching mice.[11]

The same year proved to be Brooks's artistic turning point. Both husband and wife attended an all-black poetry-writing class at a local community center. The teacher was a wealthy white socialite named Inez Cunningham Stark, who loved poetry. Every week she arrived for class

This photo of the poetry class at the Southside Community Arts Center in 1942 may include some of Brooks's and Blakely's fellow students.

◆ ◆ ◆ ◆ ◆

wearing a designer dress and hat, her red hair elegantly styled, arms full of books.

Stark would announce the evening's topic and read the poems she had chosen to illustrate it. Then the students would light into the discussion. Each would present an original poem for the others to critique. The students practiced brutal honesty. "Many a young woman went home crying; many a young man went home mad," Brooks said. "It was very helpful."[12]

Guest lecturers came to the class at Stark's invitation, among them Langston Hughes. He praised Brooks's "The Ballad of Pearl May Lee," which would appear in her first book. Stark also held a contest for her students, paying for the awards from her own pocket. "I got third place," said Henry Blakely later. "You can guess who got first!"[13]

Stark urged her students to enter other contests as well. Brooks spied a notice in the newspaper for the 1943 Midwestern Writers Conference poetry contest and entered. One Saturday morning, Brooks answered a knock at her apartment door. A disoriented-looking elderly white woman stood there. She was looking for the poetry contest winner, Gwendolyn Brooks, to give her the award and $25. "She said

"This class of hers was very alive. We were encouraged to tear each other to pieces. . . . Some people went home crying, but they always came back."[14]

Gwendolyn Brooks and Langston Hughes in 1949.
Hughes included Brooks's work in his award-winning
collection of poetry.

that she was shocked to discover that I was a Negro," Brooks said later, surprised that seeing the all-black neighborhood had not tipped the lady off.[15]

The following year, 1944, Brooks won the contest again. She entered a third time in 1945. That year the prize was awarded publicly in a ceremony at Chicago's Northwestern University. Brooks attended and heard the announcer

> After they met again at Inez Stark's poetry class, Brooks and Langston Hughes became good friends.

call her name. Too stunned to believe she had won three times, she sat silent and motionless. "You'd better come up here, Gwendolyn," the announcer teased, "or I'll give the prize to someone else."[16] She stood up, and a gasp rose from the audience when they saw she was African American. Then they burst into applause.

Brooks had already been approached by the Alfred A. Knopf company, which published Langston Hughes's books. She sent them forty poems on subjects ranging from love to nature. An editor wrote back that she had been most impressed by the poems portraying African-American life. Would Brooks contact her again when she had a book's worth?

Writer Richard Wright was impressed
with Brooks's poetry and called her a "real poet."

Chapter 6

Portrait of Bronzeville

hortly before winning the poetry contest for the third time, Brooks had sold four poems to the prestigious journal *Poetry*. This gave her the courage to resubmit her work to a book publisher. But she did not try Knopf again. Fearing what she called a "jinx," she made a list of desirable publishers and started at the top.[1] Harper and Brothers was her first choice.

Elizabeth Lawrence, a Harper editor, wrote back to say they wished to put Brooks under contract to develop a book of poems. Along with the acceptance letter, the editor sent Brooks a critique of her work by Richard Wright. A Harper author himself, Wright was the era's most prominent African-American fiction writer. "She is a real poet," Wright wrote. "She knows what to say and how to say it. . . . America needs a voice like hers."[2]

Gwendolyn Brooks had submitted nineteen poems to Harper. Most of them had been written during the burst of creativity inspired by Stark's poetry class. Brooks named the collection *A Street in Bronzeville*.

Where is Bronzeville? Is it a real place? Brooks was often asked questions like these. In the 1940s, Bronzeville was the nickname of the largest black neighborhood on the South Side of Chicago, where her family lived. In those days it was "well defined; I know," said Brooks.[3] It seemed as if an invisible line separated black and white neighborhoods. If she and her son crossed this line when they were out walking, they might have objects thrown at them by racist whites.

Many of the poems are word portraits of people she knew and events she had seen while growing up in Chicago. In "A Song in the Front Yard," Brooks took a sly dig at her mother, who required her to come home at 8:45 on a summer evening when other children played on. "Really happened!" she said about another poem, "The Vacant Lot."[4] Others she imagined as occurring on a street like hers. Her corner apartment faced two streets. "I could look first on one side and then the other. There was my material," she said.[5]

Many of the poems told stories. In later years, Brooks believed this accounted for the book's lasting popularity. "A surprising number of people can be trapped into a book of verse if there's the promise of a story," she said.[6]

"The Ballad of Pearl May Lee" tells the tale of a black man falsely accused of rape by his white girlfriend. A series of poems about a maid named Hattie Scott takes the maid through a day in which she refuses to let anyone get her down. Feminist literary critics would one day credit Brooks as one of the first to treat the lives of everyday women as subjects for serious poetry.

Richard Wright had advised Harper to group her poems around a longer poem, which would serve as a centerpiece. He also suggested that she finish with poetry that was more personal. Brooks liked this advice. Her editor, Elizabeth Lawrence, wrote that she should take her time crafting these new poems, even one or two years. "But I couldn't take my time," Brooks said.[7]

She wrote in a white heat, abandoning all parties and movies until she finished. Her centerpiece poem, "The Sundays of Satin-Legs Smith," probed the life of a dandy whose elegant wardrobe masks his lack of purpose. She dedicated a series of poems about soldiers in the ongoing war to her brother, Raymond, who was on active duty.

Brooks sent the new poems to Lawrence and waited for her response. When a letter from Harper arrived in the mail, Brooks flew to the bathroom the Blakelys shared with another family and locked herself in. She ripped the envelope open. Her editor loved the new poems and would put her book out promptly.

Nine months later, a box arrived in the mail for her. It held ten copies of *A Street in Bronzeville*. Brooks removed one of the books. "I turned the pages of the thin little thing, over and over," she said later. "My Book."[8] The official publication date in August 1945 fell on the same day World War II ended.

The first review appeared in the following Sunday's *Chicago Tribune*. On the way home from their regular Saturday night movie, she and her husband stopped to buy an early edition. By the light of a street lamp, they tore the paper open. "Chicago Can Take Pride in New Young Voice in Poetry," the headline said. Side by side, they read the entire review. Then, "in ecstasy," Brooks said, they closed the paper to wait for the bus home.[9] Another reviewer called her "a remarkable young poet . . . original . . . dynamic."[10]

A Street in Bronzeville sold well for a book of poetry but did not earn its author much money. Brooks was grateful to win a $1,000 grant from the American Academy of Arts and Letters. This was followed by grants from the Guggenheim Foundation two years in a row.

She was also named one of ten women of the year by *Mademoiselle* magazine in 1945. Though the honor did not pay anything, it was rare at this time for a popular women's magazine to take any note of nonwhites. The citation hailed *A Street in Bronzeville* as an original and realistic picture of street corner life.[11]

Many other poets supplemented their writing income by teaching college courses and giving poetry readings. Not having a college degree herself, Brooks could not teach. With the open job discrimination of the time, many universities would have refused her a job because of race, even if she did have a degree. Brooks gave a few local readings but could not travel farther because of her young son.

During their work on *A Street in Bronzeville*, Elizabeth Lawrence had asked Brooks how she fit her writing schedule into her responsibilities as a wife and mother. Brooks answered that often she would drop the "mop, broom, soap, iron or carrot grater to write down a line, or a word."[12] Sometimes, Henry would come home from school early and find her still writing at the kitchen table. Her intense concentration and furious typing always impressed him.

Henry was a personable child who liked to paint and write his own poems and stories. He was very close to his Brooks grandparents and stayed with them when his parents went out. His grandfather

"A poem rarely comes whole and completely dressed. As a rule, it comes in bits and pieces. You get an impression of something—you feel something, you anticipate something, and you begin, feebly, to put these [into] . . . words."[13]

Brooks was constantly juggling her time between writing and parenting. Both jobs had plenty of challenges—and rewards.

delighted him with stories and games. Henry had a mischievous streak and once got sent to stand in the corner for bringing his mother a bouquet of tulips that had been plucked without permission from their neighbors' gardens. One of his mother's fondest memories was of her son saying goodnight—a thousand times, it seemed—to everything and everyone in their apartment, including his puppy Cocoa and his fish Water Boy.

The Blakelys loved to give and attend parties. Though the elder Henry Blakely worked hard all day, he was never too tired for an evening's social engagement. Young Henry also liked to meet and talk to his parents' guests. At a memorable party for Langston Hughes, seventy-five guests squeezed into their kitchenette. "Nobody had a better time than Langston Hughes," Brooks said. He "was real 'folk.'"[14] On another occasion, Hughes dropped by unexpectedly. The Blakelys shared their meal of ham hocks, mustard greens, and candied sweet potatoes with him. "Just what I want!" Hughes said.[15]

Brooks had been working for some time on a series of poems about the life of an African-American woman. When she sent the collection to Harper in March 1948, her editor reacted with surprise. The poems showed Brooks experimenting with a much more formal and difficult style than she had previously used. Harper accepted the new collection, soon to be named *Annie Allen*, but with some misgivings. "You [are] a writer of rare talent and an authentic poet," Elizabeth Lawrence wrote. But while she called some of the new poems "downright exciting," others she considered obscure.[16]

Brooks agreed to revise and refine her work. She defended her new style, however. With these poems she said "exactly what I meant," using "more careful language."[17] Brooks worked on the revisions for ten months. *Annie Allen* was published in August 1949.

The reviewers immediately recognized the book's brilliance. Langston Hughes perceived what Brooks aimed to do with language. She "boil[s] her lines down to the sparest expression of the greatest meaning," he wrote. He admitted that the book was less straightforward than her previous work, and required "careful reading."[18] Poet Phyllis McGinley, in *The New York Times*, called its centerpiece poem *The Anniad* "full of insight and wisdom and pity, technically dazzling." The poem's difficulty did not dismay McGinley. On the contrary, she praised its "sophistication of thought and phrase."[19]

Then came the Pulitzer Prize. "So permanent—so irrevocable—so final," a friend wrote to Brooks.[20] For the rest of her years, she would always be known as the first African-American winner. She might as well call herself Gwendolyn "PULL-itzer" Brooks, she later joked.[21]

The prize did change her life. New opportunities in writing and, eventually, teaching opened up to her. But the United States was still a racially segregated society

"Changing tenants" was a coded way of saying that whites had to move out. Then the apartments would be rented only to blacks.

in 1950. Winning did not accord her the level of fame and prosperity that it would have given a white poet.

Just as her professional life reached new heights, lack of money and housing discrimination turned Brooks's personal life into "scrambled eggs," she said.[22] Chicago housing, including apartment buildings, was rigidly segregated at that time. A landlord would not allow even one black family to move into a building with whites. Instead, he would evict all the white tenants and solicit all-new black tenants. Between 1940 and 1950, Chicago's black population doubled, from a quarter million to a half million. Traditionally black neighborhoods burst at the seams. Yet whenever a black family managed to find housing on a street previously regarded as "white," racial conflict broke out. Nine major race riots rocked the city from 1945 to 1954.

To save money, the Blakelys had begun to share a house with a woman they knew. Brooks became the object of gossip from other women in the neighborhood. They could not understand that, as a writer, she worked at home. They criticized her for being lazy and not contributing to her family.

Brooks demanded that they find a new place to live. Blakely refused. The couple separated once again. Brooks and her son moved briefly to Kalamazoo, Michigan, the town her Aunt Eppie had lived in. The Blakelys had recently had the opportunity to buy a house there cheaply, and they rented it out for the income. Part of the house was empty, however, and mother and son settled there.

Quickly it became apparent that this would be no better. Young Henry was told that he would have to repeat a grade, strictly on the assumption that Chicago schools were not as good as Kalamazoo's. The tenants rebelled at having their landlady so close by. Brooks and her son moved back to Chicago.

Still, the Blakelys were forced to live apart, unable to find accommodation for the three of them. The elder Henry slept at his garage. Gwendolyn and her son took an apartment in a neighborhood rougher than any she had ever lived in. For Brooks, this was the lowest period of her married life. At last, they found a suitable place, for $100 a month, a very high rent at that time. They sacrificed to reunite the family.

Chapter 7

"Poets Who Are Negroes"

In the United States of 1950, African Americans were denied full citizenship rights. Employers in the North openly practiced discrimination. Newspaper ads for low-paying, menial jobs would read HELP WANTED—COLORED MALE or HELP WANTED—COLORED FEMALE. African-American students were often pushed into vocational courses and discouraged from striving for college. Many restaurants and hotels refused African-American customers.

In the South, it was even worse. States from Delaware to Texas operated separate, unequal school systems—one for whites and an inferior one for blacks. All buses, trains, restaurants, hotels, restrooms, and even water fountains were segregated. Almost everywhere in the South, only white people could register to vote, despite the fact that the U.S. Constitution had guaranteed black men this right nearly a hundred years before.

Most northern whites took a casual attitude toward this injustice. Presidential candidate Dwight D. Eisenhower was quoted in a magazine as predicting that African Americans would have full citizenship rights—by the year 2000.[1] But when Eisenhower was elected in 1952, he would get a surprise. African Americans would not wait.

The NAACP had been pursuing a legal strategy for ending segregation for some time. The lawsuits that would become known as *Brown* v. *Board of Education of Topeka, Kansas* were already wending their way through the justice system. In 1954, the U.S. Supreme Court would rule in *Brown* that racially separate school systems were unconstitutional. One year later, a black seamstress and civil rights activist named Rosa Parks would refuse to give up her seat to a white man on a bus in Montgomery, Alabama. Ordinary African Americans like Parks would begin to demand their rights in an unprecedented way.

Gwendolyn Brooks had led a life relatively sheltered from racial prejudice. Her loving and fiercely protective parents had taught her to accept all races. Her negative experiences attending Hyde Park Branch High School and seeking housing had not turned her against whites. She considered herself an integrationist, favoring a society in which all races would live together in harmony.

Since breaking into publication, Brooks had made many white acquaintances in the literary world. She picked up some additional income reviewing books for Chicago newspapers and magazines whose editors had become her friends. She attended parties, book signings, and writers' conferences, often finding that she and her husband were the only African Americans present.

When Brooks won the Pulitzer Prize, the prestigious Society of Mid-Land Authors gave her a tea party that she described as "exquisite" and welcomed her as a new member. She was well aware, though, that they had never noticed her before the honor.[2] This was subtle discrimination compared to an incident in New York City. On a visit with her former teacher, Inez

The 1950s

The Great Depression ended with the United States' entry into World War II. Industries were revitalized and the economy turned around. The years after the war were a time of prosperity for America.

Once again, however, blacks did not benefit as much as whites. As white war veterans and their families flocked to new houses in the suburbs, blacks were kept out. As whites obtained good jobs in the booming economy, blacks continued to face discrimination.

The nation was changing. American teens embraced a rebellious rock-and-roll youth culture. Television and other inventions brought new technology into people's homes. And African Americans stood up to demand equality through the civil rights movement.

Stark, Brooks was turned away from the hotel where they attempted to register.

In 1950, Brooks had published an article on her artistic beliefs in *Phylon*, an African-American scholarly journal. "Poets who are Negroes," she wrote, have dramatic, moving, important subject matter ready at hand by virtue of their race. Still, she argued, merely presenting the facts of racial injustice does not result in art. Art requires "interpretation" and "subtlety." She concluded, "The Negro poet's most urgent duty, at present, is to polish his technique, his way of presenting his truths and his beauties, that these may be more . . . overwhelming."[3]

Brooks knew that whites bought most of her books and attended most of her poetry readings. When she wrote, she knew whites were the main part of her audience.[4] Over the next twenty years, as the civil rights and black power movements progressed, Brooks would retain some of her beliefs about the races, and she would change others. She and America were both about to undergo a revolution.

❖ ❖ ❖

Shortly after the family reunited, Brooks discovered that she was

> "At the present time, poets who happen also to be Negroes are twice-tried. They have to write poetry, and they have to remember that they are Negroes."[5]

Early in her career, Brooks considered herself an integrationist,
favoring a society in which all races would live together in harmony.

pregnant with her second child. Eleven-year-old Henry Blakely III eagerly awaited the birth of his first sibling. "All my friends at school talk about their brothers or sisters and I haven't got anything," he grumbled. He did not care whether the baby would be a boy or girl. "I know it will be cute," he said.[6]

Brooks firmly believed she would have a girl, and she was right. Nora Brooks Blakely was born on September 8, 1951. This time Brooks made it safely to the hospital. The newborn Nora cried the whole night through for two nights. After that, she stopped and barely ever cried again.

The eleven-year gap between their two children caused the elder Henry Blakely to feel almost as if they had two firstborns. By now, Brooks was a relaxed and confident mother. "I squeezed, kissed, grabbed [my children] on sudden impulse," she said. She carried Nora around so much of the time, her husband complained, "Why don't you put that child down?"[7]

The birth of her daughter revived Brooks's longtime dream of owning a house of their own. Brooks's parents had bought their home when she was only four years old. Most of her childhood had been centered on the warm, loving atmosphere her parents had painstakingly created there. It hurt Brooks that she had not been able to recreate such deep roots for her own family.

Buying a house would require a sizable down payment. The Blakelys had never been able to earn and save enough to have such a large sum at one time. How could Brooks come up with enough money to buy a house? Elizabeth Lawrence, Brooks's editor at Harper, had often urged her to try writing fiction. Lawrence had pointed out that even the best poetry commanded only a small, select audience. Fiction, on the other hand, had the potential to sell more. So the publisher would offer a larger advance payment. The money would be just what Brooks needed to buy a home.

Despite having a new baby at home, Brooks set right to work. She pulled out a group of short stories she had written years before, tentatively titled *American Family Brown*. She refocused these stories around one character, a young woman named Maud Martha. Shortly after her daughter Nora's first birthday, she submitted the manuscript to Elizabeth Lawrence. Harper offered Brooks a contract with an advance payment of $500, five times what she had received for *Annie Allen*.

More people would buy books of fiction than poetry collections. So Brooks set to work on a novel.

The house hunt began. So determined was Brooks not to fritter away the $500 on small expenses that she left the check uncashed for months. Finally Lawrence told her that the uncashed check was causing problems for Harper bookkeepers. The Blakelys sold the property they rented out in

Michigan. After a long search, they found the house they wanted, a small, brown, one-story on Chicago's South Evans Avenue.

They took the money they had squirreled away, added loans from a friend and David and Keziah Brooks, borrowed mortgage money from a bank, and then—the house was theirs. They moved in on October 10, 1953, young Henry's thirteenth birthday. Even though they were finally settled, making the monthly mortgage payment to the bank was not easy. Henry Blakely temporarily gave up working in his own business and became a foreman in a truck factory to earn more.

Meanwhile, *Maud Martha* had been published two weeks before. In form, this novel was ahead of its time. The highly poetic language offered brief glimpses—snapshots, almost—of the life of a young, African-American woman in Chicago. Many reviewers did not know what to make of the book. Others recognized it for the work of genius that it was. "In technique and impression it stands virtually alone of its kind," said one.[8] "A superb achievement," said another.[9]

Brooks admitted that *Maud Martha* was heavily auto-biographical but said that she had "twisted" reality. Its heroine is a "nicer" and "better coordinated" person than its author, she said wryly.[10] She took pleasure at having sketched many Chicago scenes with precision and remembered her husband's embarrassment when she pulled out a pad and pencil in a nightclub to make notes.

Though *Maud Martha* did not at the time sell as well as Brooks or her publisher had hoped, it has remained her most popular book. African-American feminist literary critics now hold it in particularly high esteem, both as art and as a pioneering portrayal of a woman's life.

In her novel, *Maud Martha,* Brooks "twisted" reality to turn her own life into fiction.

When Elizabeth Lawrence visited the Blakelys the following year, she found their family and new home delightful. Nora, a preschooler, was the darling of the household. "Tell me a 'tory," she demanded over and over again.[11] Brooks delighted in obliging her, particularly by sharing stories her father had told her. Not surprisingly, Nora taught herself to read at an early age. With such a charming and precocious child to care for, Brooks struggled to carve out one hour a day for her writing.

When Henry graduated from eighth grade, everyone in the auditorium heard Nora echo the principal's words, and then add some of her own. "He-wy—'owington—Bwaky," she piped up. "Here—come—HEHwy!"[12] Despite the age gap, the siblings adored each other. Still, they bickered like any brother and sister. One day, when Nora lay ill with the chicken pox, they began to quarrel. Their father had to separate them. He told Henry that he should not hit his sick sister. "No-o," the boy replied, "but I can credit it to her account."[13]

Young Henry's parents encouraged him to think for himself. They expected their son to examine and challenge issues others might take for granted. When he began taking science courses in high school, his imagination caught fire. His once indifferent grades soared. He won numerous prizes in science fairs and competitions.

Around the same time, Henry tested the boundaries of his strict parents a bit. He decided to stay and see a movie twice, arriving home much later than expected. To his surprise, he found his normally calm mother so worried that she wept uncontrollably.[14]

She and her husband knew better than Henry the dangers that faced African-American boys. In 1955, Chicago was rocked by the torture and murder of one of its own: fourteen-year-old Emmett Till. The Chicago teenager had been visiting relatives in rural Mississippi when, allegedly, he whistled at a white woman. The whites in town knew that the woman's husband killed Till in retaliation—and they approved. An all-white jury promptly acquitted the husband of the crime. Brooks could not help but imagine her own son in this situation.[15]

During the remainder of the 1950s, Brooks published only one book, a collection of children's poetry titled *Bronzeville Boys and Girls*. Family life swallowed much of her time. In addition, she spent years developing a novel for teens and a biography of African-American poet Phillis Wheatley in verse, only to leave both books unfinished.

Then the burgeoning civil rights movement inspired Brooks to begin work on a new selection of poems. Many of them would address subjects straight from the headlines. Brooks imagined the emotions of two women, Emmett Till's mother and the wife of his murderer, in "A Bronzeville Mother Loiters in Mississippi. Meanwhile, a Mississippi Mother Burns Bacon." She pictured a reporter puzzled over how to explain the violent white reaction to school integration in "The *Chicago Defender* Sends a Man to Little Rock." In "The Ballad of Rudolph

Brooks based some of her new poems on the news headlines of the day.

Reed," her hero is a black husband and father defending his family's new home from rock-throwing whites.

One day, Brooks passed by a neighborhood pool hall and observed seven young men, apparently playing hooky from school. "I wondered how they felt about themselves," she said. "I decided . . . they were insecure. They were not cherished by the society." The poem they inspired, "We Real Cool," became her best-loved and most widely reprinted work.

Years later, she visited a Washington, D.C., high school to read her poetry. When she began to recite "We Real Cool," the students all "jumped up . . . chanting that poem, snapping their fingers rhythmically. I loved that," she said.[16]

Around this time, David Brooks's health began to fail. He underwent an operation for heart and stomach problems, which turned out to be incurable. On November 21, 1959, at home with his family surrounding him, he asked that the window of his bedroom be closed, for he felt cold. When this was done, his wife took his hand and spoke gently to him. Minutes later, he died peacefully. Gwendolyn Brooks mourned her father deeply and put her grief into a poem, "In Honor of David Anderson Brooks, My Father." Later, this poem served as the dedication of her new book *The Bean Eaters*.

The title of this volume echoed a painting by Vincent Van Gogh called "The Potato Eaters," which portrays a poor, elderly couple sharing a meager meal. Published in early 1960, *The Bean Eaters* received mixed reviews. A few reviewers felt that Brooks's poems about racial injustice failed as art. Others found them "fresh and frightening . . . true to the finest achievements in contemporary poetry."[17] Brooks later felt these reviews marked the point at which she fell out of favor with most of the white literary establishment. She imagined them saying "Watch it, Miss Brooks," and claiming she was "getting too social."[18] They were right. She soon would become very "social" indeed.

Chapter 8

Time of the Tall Walkers

"It is difficult to see Gwendolyn Brooks, the Pulitzer prize winning poet, when you are looking at Gwendolyn Brooks, the woman," wrote a friend, the African-American novelist Frank London Brown. In his 1961 magazine profile, Brown highlighted her dual roles: ordinary wife and mother, extraordinary writer. He described her walking to the market with a shopping bag. He noticed that at a gathering of male writers, she said little and silently emptied the overflowing ashtrays without being asked. He also noted that, with intense creativity, she sometimes woke up in the dead of night to jot an idea on scratch paper. Brown found himself baffled, wondering if such a fine writer could really be "'just a Chicago housewife,'" as she claimed.[1]

As Brooks continued to juggle her roles as writer and homemaker, strife again struck her family. After her son,

Henry, graduated from high school, he began college at the University of Illinois, then transferred to Chicago's Roosevelt University. The nineteen-year-old lived at home and tussled with his parents over the house rules. He was running with a fast crowd, they thought. His girlfriend and the parties he attended were too wild. When a family argument boiled over, the young man moved out. His parents put on a calm, brave front, trusting they had given him a firm foundation in life. Only Nora, who idolized her brother, gave in to heartbreak. She cried uncontrollably for two days. Not long afterward, Henry left college and joined the Marines.[2]

In the early 1960s, lack of money still plagued the Blakelys. The elder Henry had resumed running his own insurance business, winning several important contracts. Brooks, however, continued to make only a pittance from writing. She earned a mere $100 from her publisher as an advance payment for *The Bean Eaters*. It was exactly what she had received for *Annie Allen* twelve years before. Then *The Bean Eaters* sold less than two thousand copies, the fewest of all her books for Harper.

In 1961, Frank London Brown attempted to persuade Roosevelt University to hire Brooks as a teacher. They declined, citing her lack of a college degree. But the next year, he succeeded in engaging her to lead a class on American literature for trade union members. The course was part of a special leadership program that Brown ran at

"I could look first on one side and then the other. There was my material," said Brooks about the streets of Chicago, pictured here in the early 1960s.

the University of Chicago. Finally, Chicago's Columbia College offered her a permanent position teaching poetry and fiction writing in 1963.

At first, Brooks hesitated to call the job teaching. "Helping? lightly leading? surely not teaching!" she speculated. She bought herself a good blue suit to wear for class. She considered herself strict and thorough but innovative in the classroom. She had her students listen to recordings of poets reciting their work. They acted out verse plays and staged debates and panel discussions. More than anything else, she required them to "read and read and read and write and write and write," she said.[3] During the remainder of the decade, Brooks would teach part-time at several colleges.

The Civil Rights Movement

African Americans were standing up for their rights in the courts, in the press, and on the streets since before the Civil War. Still, historians agree that the modern civil rights movement picked up speed in the 1940s. The National Association for the Advancement of Colored People (NAACP) began chipping away at segregation by filing—and winning—many small lawsuits. The armed forces were integrated in 1948. *Brown* v. *Board of Education*, the Montgomery bus boycott, and the murder of innocent young Emmett Till made headlines in the mid-fifties. Suddenly, white Northerners could see the shame of segregation in action on television. Civil rights organizations like the NAACP, Martin Luther King, Jr.'s Southern Christian Leadership Conference, and the Student Nonviolent Coordinating Committee seized the moment. At the same time, by joining sit-ins, voter registration drives, marches, and other protests, ordinary African Americans—students, teachers, maids, and clerks— became part of the movement.

Experience at the head of a class gave Brooks more confidence as a public speaker. The newsworthiness of the civil rights movement increased the demand for Brooks to lecture and read her poetry about African-American life. Having one child grown and the second in school enabled her to travel more.

Ten-year-old Nora, who had also begun to write, prepared a news story about one of her mother's appearances, an "expense-paid trip to COLORADO." Nora wrote with a poet's feel for the spacing of words on the page.

"She is very dedicated to her work   poetry   so she deserves this trip I feel. I'm left   with a strange sort of   nice   father. Who is strict but good."[4]

In 1963, with Brooks's income from teaching and public appearances, and Blakely's insurance business, the family finances at last became secure.

That same year, Harper published *Selected Poems*. Brooks and her editor Elizabeth Lawrence had chosen these poems as the best from her first three books. The volume also included several new poems on the civil rights movement, her most militant work yet. "Riders to the Blood Red Wrath" honored the achievements of the Freedom Riders, young people both black and white who had withstood beatings, firebombing, and arrest to change the segregation laws for interstate buses.

In 1964, Brooks wrote that black and white poets must see things differently, even things like raindrops and sunlight.

A black poet might see raindrops as "racial tears," she suggested. "The golden sun might remind them that they are burning."[5] The civil rights movement reached its peak that year. In Chicago, activists focused on employment discrimination. Even in all-black areas, the jobs at neighborhood stores went to whites. This was true at Brooks's local supermarket. When young people in her neighborhood decided to picket the store, demanding that it hire without discrimination, they asked Brooks to help. At this point, she was not willing to resume an activist role (though she had picketed against lynching back in her twenties). However, she did write the letter that activists sent to the store's owner, demanding equality in hiring. When the owners refused, the pickets went up, and shoppers turned elsewhere. Loss of business succeeded in forcing the owners to hire African-American employees for the first time.

> Brooks wrote that black poets and white poets see the world differently.

In the South, white resistance to the civil rights movement had turned increasingly violent. The Freedom Rides had been followed by mass jailings. The historic March on Washington had been followed by a church bombing that killed four black Alabama girls attending Sunday school. The passage of the Civil Rights Act was followed by the murders of civil rights workers in Mississippi and Alabama. As violence against African-American activists increased, Brooks had come to believe that the relationship between the races would be "getting worse before it gets better."[6]

Still, some things were gradually changing. President Lyndon B. Johnson invited Brooks to the White House for a Scholars' Reception. She fretted over what to wear, settling on a blue chiffon gown. Brooks reasoned that a writer should wear her best to meet the president. But when she arrived at the affair, she felt momentary embarrassment that the other women wore suits and dresses. She met the first lady and the famous attorney Thurgood Marshall, whom the president would appoint to the Supreme Court as the nation's first African-American Justice. At last, Brooks had her chance to shake the president's hand, only to find herself "tongue-tied" in response to his "handsome smile," she said.[7]

For her next book, Brooks returned to the experience that continued to haunt her, working in the Mecca Building for the phony preacher Dr. French. For years, she had wrestled creatively with turning this period of her life into art. In 1954, Ursula Nordstrom, head of children's publishing at Harper, had invited her to submit a novel for young people. Brooks had spent several years writing an autobiographical novel for teens about the Mecca, but finally abandoned it, unsatisfied.

Now she proposed to Elizabeth Lawrence a single epic poem of two thousand words. Brooks envisioned a poetic "mosaic" of the lives of the Mecca's more than one thousand tenants. The reader would meet them and learn their stories as the main character, a poor single parent named Mrs. Sally, searched the building frantically for her missing daughter Pepita. Brooks aimed, she said, to create a work of "music," "color," "horror," "mystery."[8]

In the spring of 1967, Brooks set off for a poetry reading tour of college campuses. By this time, the civil rights movement had been going strong for more than a decade. The Voting Rights Act of 1965 and several U.S. Supreme Court decisions had ruled against legalized segregation in the South. But full equality of blacks with whites had not automatically followed. Violence and white resistance to change had persisted. Many young African-American civil rights activists grew frustrated. They expelled white members from their civil rights organization, the Student Nonviolent Coordinating Committee, known as SNCC. They initiated a Black Power movement that urged its members to take up arms in self-defense.

Brooks's next-to-last stop on her tour was at nearly all-white South Dakota State College. The audience there "loved" her, she said.[9] Next, she headed for a Black Writers' Conference at the historically black Fisk University in Nashville, Tennessee. She was tired from the tour, she recalled, and thought she could "whiz through Fisk, give my little reading" and go home.[10]

As soon as she arrived, however, she immediately

During the 1960s, Brooks was inspired by the civil rights movement, and her poetry became more "social."

sensed something new, something important in the air. The young African Americans in attendance gave speeches, read their poetry, and performed their music with new fervor. They seemed "proud and so committed to their own people," she said.[11] They showed no fear challenging, even ridiculing, the prominent adult authors who gave readings and speeches. Brooks felt her own reading aroused merely cold respect. Perplexed, but fascinated, she drank it all in for two days. She did not understand everything she saw, but quickly what she called a "hot sureness" took hold of her. She knew she had witnessed the birth of a new type of black artist, a "tall walker," she said, unafraid of white opinion, embracing black power.[12]

The young writers believed that "black poets should write as blacks, about blacks, and address themselves to blacks," she said.[13] She had not done this in her own writing, she realized, and resolved to change. With chagrin, she recalled a famous poem of hers that had pleaded with whites to acknowledge that blacks were human. Never again would she stoop to such poetic "whining," she decided. In the future, her poems would speak to blacks "without frill and without fear of the white presence."[14]

For the rest of her life, Brooks regarded 1967 as the transition year of her artistic journey and the Fisk Writers' Conference as its watershed event. She returned to Chicago contemplating all she had seen and learned. She determined to live and write differently, but how? The answer would come more quickly than she imagined.

Chapter 9

Into the Whirlwind

Nora Blakely saw the change as soon as her mother arrived home. Brooks walked "three feet in the air," her daughter said.[1] A telegram lay in the middle of the dining room table when Brooks came home from Nashville. Chicago musician Oscar Brown Jr. had invited her to a preview performance of an original musical called *Opportunity Knocks*. Brooks took Nora to the show, which was sung, danced, and acted by members of a large and notorious Chicago street gang, the Blackstone Rangers. Brooks said the talent on stage "electrified" her.[2]

She felt a "yearning" to do something for the gang members. "Are there any writers among them?" she asked Walter Bradford, a poet and community organizer who had worked with the Rangers.[3] Indeed there were. In fact, learning that Brooks would see their performance, the young poets had asked if they could meet with her. Bradford arranged for Brooks to lead a poetry workshop at the same Presbyterian church that had hosted the musical.

The next Friday night, seven or eight Rangers faced Brooks in the church basement. She began to teach the same way she taught her college poetry classes. The Rangers stared at her. "They didn't know what in the world I was 'about'," she said.[4]

The following week, perhaps one Ranger remained for her class. The rest drifted back upstairs to rehearse their play. But the room filled up anyway. African-American college and high school students, who had heard about the workshop through the grapevine, replaced them.

One of the workshop members was twenty-four-year-old Don L. Lee. The previous year, Lee had self-published his first book, *Think Black*, and hawked it for $1 a copy on the Chicago streets. Lee described his first sight of Brooks: "There was this . . . rather small woman behind this table, and she was talking about poetry. [Immediately], "we drew to each other like oxygen and hydrogen." When still a teenager, Lee had lost his own mother, an alcoholic and drug-abuser. Brooks quickly became his "cultural mother," as he called her.[5]

Once again, Brooks began to teach, and once again, she stopped. These young people "did not want me to 'teach' them anything about the sonnet form," she said.

Instead, the group quickly became simply a gathering of friends talking about poetry and reading their work to each other.[6]

Soon the workshops moved to Brooks's home. Every month she held an open house for young poets and other artists in four-hour marathon sessions. The meals she served fed many a hungry student for the day. The young people expressed their gratitude toward Brooks to an interviewer who profiled her for a magazine. They did not thank Brooks directly, but "cherished" her nonetheless, they said.[7] She nourished them with her guidance as well. "Gwen's wonderful and motherly," one said, "but when it gets down to working on paper, she's formidable."[8]

Brooks sparred more than once with Don Lee over his use of profanity in his poems. He resisted her criticism and even "stormed out of her house one day," he said. Brooks felt using a curse took the lazy way, rather than digging for a better, more precise word. Lee eventually grew to see the wisdom in her point of view. "She was testy about bad language," he said, "and about laziness— not just laziness in writing, but laziness in one's person. She was always trying to push for the best."[9]

The group often discussed current events and debated social issues as well as poetry. The young people suggested books for Brooks to read, such as *The Autobiography of Malcolm X* and W. E. B. Du Bois's *The Souls of Black Folk*. Brooks had already rethought her views on writing for a black audience. Slowly, she began to rethink her views on integration and black/white relations in society.

Gradually, Brooks began to see herself as naïve in thinking that "all we had to do was keep on appealing to the whites to help us and they would." She said she lost her faith in integration as "the solution." Instead, she came to subscribe to the black power belief that black people should support each other and build their own institutions. Blacks should start their own schools, the-aters, and publishing houses, rather than struggle against white resistance to become part of the white world. Brooks even dropped most of her white friends and literary acquaintances. "My people are black people," she said. "It is to them that I appeal for understanding."[10] Still, precise as ever about her choice of words, she was careful to tell interviewers that her new stance was not "*against* white, but FOR black."[11]

Henry Blakely did not agree with his wife's new point of view. He remained an integrationist. He pointed out that, as a businessman, he had for years advocated community support of African-American institutions. Brooks had always appreciated the ease with which she could discuss any issue with her husband. Now their debates grew hotter.

Meanwhile, Brooks and her group of young writers began to promote their poetry in unconventional ways and bring it directly to the people. The poets often read their work aloud in Chicago's Malcolm X Park, their new name for the former "Washington" Park. One day, the group entered a tavern. Brooks said that Don Lee strode to the front of the barroom, announced, "Look, folks, we're gonna lay some poetry on you," and began to recite.[12] The drinkers turned around on their stools, listened, and even applauded. The other poets took turns reciting. Brooks contributed her crowd-pleasing "We Real Cool."

The high point of the group's public performances,

The Black Arts Movement

Along with New York City and the San Francisco Bay area, Chicago was one of the hotbeds of the "Black Arts Movement," which thrived from the mid-1960s to the mid-1970s. The poets, playwrights, and publishers of the movement believed that literature should reflect and serve the black liberation movement. They did not care what white critics wrote or thought. If their writing moved and inspired the black reader or audience, it had succeeded.

thought Brooks, came at the dedication of a mural called the "Wall of Respect" in Chicago. A drama group performed, musicians played, poets read. Brooks proclaimed her poetry in front of the mural portraits of great African Americans. Her own portrait was part of the mural. "To see all those black people out on the street together, loving each other," she said. "It was just wonderful."[13] Eventually, Brooks contributed an introduction to *Jump Bad*, an anthology of the workshop writers' poems.

In 1968, her next book, *In the Mecca*, was published by Harper. The title poem took up half the book. In the other half, called "After Mecca," Brooks celebrated her new beliefs. Included were poems commemorating assassinated civil rights leaders Medgar Evers and Malcolm X, and portraying the Blackstone Rangers. Most striking were two long poems addressed directly to African Americans, which she titled sermons. Poetically she preached to her people. In one poem, she urged them to take their destinies into their own hands. If they chose, they could even change the direction of a river just by telling it to turn, she said symbolically. In the other poem, she urged artists to join the struggle, to "bloom" even in the "whirlwind" of social change.[14]

In the Mecca was not reviewed as widely in the mainstream press as her previous books had been. It was nominated for the prestigious National Book Award, though it did not win. The writing was too black for the judges, thought Don Lee.[15] *In the Mecca* would be her final original work for Harper. Her longtime editor, Elizabeth Lawrence, had retired.

Brooks decided to put her beliefs into action. In the future, all her new work would be published by African-American-owned presses. The first of them, *Riot*, was a pamphlet-length poem on Chicago's civil unrest following the Martin Luther King, Jr., assassination. Dudley Randall, a poet and Brooks's close friend, published it through his Broadside Press.

The same year, the state of Illinois named Brooks its poet laureate. The previous laureate, Carl Sandberg, had held the honor for years without performing any official duties. Not surprisingly, Brooks announced that she would be a different, more activist laureate. She reached out to the children and young people of Illinois with poetry readings and writing contests. Eventually, she used her own money to fund numerous awards for the state's young poets.

GWENDOLYN BROOKS

By now, Nora Blakely was near high school graduation. White violence against blacks struck close to Brooks's family when a friend of Nora's, Kenneth Alexander, was shot and killed by white Chicago policemen. Brooks agonized over the death. She remembered seeing Kenneth seated with her daughter on the high school stage only a few months before. At the honors assembly, Kenneth, the

Chicago neighborhoods were devastated by riots after the assassination of Martin Luther King, Jr. They had not been restored by the early 1970s. Contrast this picture with the vibrant street scene shown on page 75.

only boy to win, had shyly acknowledged the audience's applause. Brooks remembered congratulating him, chatting with him at the refreshments afterward. "What do you do with dreams in a grave?" she asked.[16]

> "True black writers speak *as* blacks, *about* blacks, *to* blacks."[17]

In the late sixties, many blacks denounced hair-straightening as an unnecessary imitation of whites. The young people in Brooks's writing group urged her to adopt a "natural," or Afro, hairstyle. At first she resisted, but one day she arrived at a meeting with the new look as a surprise. The room "howled," Don Lee said.[18] Brooks never straightened her hair again.

The Blakelys again experienced turmoil in guiding a child through the teen years. Nora was an outstanding student and creative person. She grumbled that her father appreciated her cooking more than her intelligence. She thought Blakely, like many men in the days before the feminist movement, gave more importance to the achievements of men than to those of women. Brooks sided with her daughter. She and her husband also disagreed over whom and how Nora should be allowed to date. One disagreement ended in a shoving match between Nora and her father that left Brooks in tears.[19]

In December 1969, to the shock and surprise of everyone who knew them, Gwendolyn Brooks and Henry Blakely decided to separate.[20]

Chapter 10

Furious Flower

Brooks refused to offer outsiders an explanation for the couple's decision to split up. Though they had no plans to divorce, they both decided separation was "best" for them, she wrote. "That won't be enough for the reader but it is enough for me."[1] She now made enough money from her poetry readings and lectures to give up teaching. Writing, promoting poetry, and the black liberation movement became her top priorities.

The freedom of being single suited Brooks just fine. She could read, write, cook, and do housework entirely as she pleased now. Or not do them. She found she loved the peace and solitude of living alone. Nora had left for the University of Illinois, where she was an honor student. Brooks and her daughter remained exceptionally close, as they would all their lives.

Brooks was not as close, however, to her son, who was married and working with computers. Some of that void was filled by her love for Walter Bradford and Don Lee. "They have been more like sons to me than my own son," she said, "the way a mother dreams of—affectionate, [with] a sharing of ideas."[2]

Family Pictures, published in 1970, was Brooks's first full book published by the African-American-owned Broadside Press. The poems celebrated Brooks's belief in the familyhood of all people of African descent. In the poem "Paul Robeson," she wrote that "we are each other's business."[3] *The World of Gwendolyn Brooks*, published the following year, was her last book published by Harper's. It included all five of her Harper books: four volumes of poetry and her novel *Maud Martha*. Brooks had to fight for the inclusion of *In the Mecca*.

Ebony magazine asked Brooks to visit Montgomery, Alabama, to report on changes in the city since the 1955 bus boycott. Her 1971 article united her with the only other African American at that time who had won a Pulitzer Prize. Photographer Moneta Sleet had won the award for his photography during the civil rights movement. Brooks wrote the article in verse, and Sleet provided the pictures.

Shortly afterward, Brooks made the trip she had longed for—to Africa. On her first day in Kenya, she exulted, "The earth of *Africa* is under my feet!"[4] Brooks recorded her mixed impressions of the country. She delighted in the low, musical voices of the Kenyan women, the warm manners and fervent handshakes of the men. The majestic wildlife at a game park lived up to her every expectation. But she was distressed that everywhere she went, people recognized her as an American and assumed she was rich. She was received by Margaret Kenyatta, the mayor of Nairobi and daughter of one of the country's founding fathers. Nora had been an exchange student the previous year at the University of Nairobi, and Brooks paid an official visit to the school.

Her next stop was Tanzania, where she thrilled to see snow-capped Mount Kilimanjaro. She had American friends living and working in the city of Dar es Salaam. This enabled her to get a better feel for everyday African life than she had in Kenya. Some of her friends were farmers, who escorted her into the back country, or "bush," which she found wild and beautiful. She took the opportunity to visit a Tanzanian family in their modest country home. She gave a poetry reading at a college and lunched with the country's premier novelist, Ayi Kwei Armah. Always, her greatest pleasure in Africa was being surrounded by black people.

That fall, the City College of New York persuaded her to return to teaching. Every week she flew back and forth to Chicago to give two poetry workshops. D. H. Melhem, who later wrote extensively on Brooks's work, was a young

African-American Literature After 1950

In 1952 Ralph Ellison, with his novel *Invisible Man*, was the first African American to win the National Book Award. James Baldwin burst onto the scene in 1954 with an autobiographical novel, *Go Tell It on the Mountain*. In the 1970s, poet/memoirists Maya Angelou and Nikki Giovanni became among the best-loved African-American writers of their generation. Other renowned fiction writers included Pulitzer Prize winners James Alan McPherson (who won in 1978) and Alice Walker (1983). Toni Morrison's steady stream of brilliant novels, starting with *The Bluest Eye* in 1970, led to her becoming the first African American to win the Nobel Prize for Literature (1993). Today, African-American authors appear regularly on the best-seller lists and win prominent literary awards. The 2004 Pulitzer Prize for fiction was awarded to African-American author Edward P. Jones.

graduate student at the time. She recorded her impressions of Brooks in the classroom: "Alert, elegant, slim, her lustrous skin a deep brown, expressive eyes and hands like those in a painting by El Greco, a woman charged with enormous vitality."[5]

By now, Brooks had become a master at public poetry readings, drawing large and excited audiences wherever she appeared. Melhem observed her extraordinary rapport with listeners at City College. Brooks introduced each poem with personal commentary, sometimes humorous, sometimes serious. But this was "no ordinary reading," Melhem thought. "It was an urgent reaching out, especially to Black members of the audience."[6]

On Christmas Day 1971, the fifty-four-year-old Brooks suffered a mild heart attack. She withdrew from her teaching commitment and its strenuous commute. Though she would teach workshops in the future, she never taught full courses again.

Report From Part One, a book of autobiographical sketches, was published in 1972 by Broadside. Like *Maud Martha*, it does not tell its story in a straightforward narrative. Instead, it takes the poet's way, using brief word pictures and poetic language. In it, Brooks wrote movingly about her childhood and youth, giving particular praise to the achievement of her parents in the face of great odds.

Her mother, Keziah Brooks, turned eighty-five in 1973. Gwendolyn planned a party to celebrate. As a surprise, she decided to invite her estranged husband, Henry Blakely, whom her mother had always loved like a son.

When she phoned to tell Henry about the event, the couple fell to chatting. He had been writing a lot of new poetry, Blakely revealed. He read some of it to his wife over the phone. The new poems were "really good," Brooks believed. "Those poems have *got* to be published," she told him. In fact, Blakely's first book, *A Windy Place*, would be published the next year. Blakely offered to take her out to eat to continue the discussion, and Brooks accepted. "We just kept going out to dinner and talking about poetry," she said.[7]

The couple reunited, much to the delight of Keziah Brooks, who had been grieved by their separation. As newlyweds, Brooks and Blakely had been too poor to afford a honeymoon trip. For their reconciliation, they took a "second" honeymoon to Ghana and England. The

Brooks always enjoyed talking to children and encouraging them to write.

◆◆◆◆◆

couple picked up their mutually enjoyable teasing and verbal sparring right where they had left off four years earlier. Throughout Ghana, they debated social issues raised by their sightseeing. They visited the cities of Accra and Kumasi. The most memorable and draining experience of the trip was to Elmina Castle, where captured Africans had been penned before being shipped as slaves to the New World. "No one—well, no Black—experiences Elmina without exhaustion, ache, rage . . . as I did, as Henry did," Brooks wrote.[8]

Brooks, who so valued family ties, was gratified to have her own family intact once more. It did not matter that her children were now in their twenties and thirties. "That's a family unit," she said. When Henry and Nora visited, "there's real happiness in the dining room." She loved the comments that came "bouncing . . . scissoring and knifing past me" as the witty brood gathered and talked.[9]

In the mid-1970s, Brooks turned much of her attention to children. *The Tiger Who Wore White Gloves* became her first picture book. The story was inspired by a Halloween costume her daughter had worn as a child. Nora had gone out to trick-or-treat but returned dissatisfied. Something was missing from her costume, but what? With the addition of white gloves, Nora felt ready to resume her holiday celebration. Brooks "crack[ed] up" with laughter at the

As Brooks read to a class of children, the librarian listened intently.

sight, Nora Blakely said, and turned the experience into a fable urging children to be true to themselves.[10]

The story was published by Third World Press. Don Lee, who had by then changed his name to Haki Madhubuti, founded this publishing house, which eventually became the longest-lived African-American publishing company in the United States. Brooks also wrote two books for children on poetry composition, *A Young Poet's Primer* and *Very Young Poets*. Both of these Brooks published herself. After Broadside Press went out of business in the mid-1970s, all her remaining books would be self-published or brought out by Third World Press.

Brooks also devoted many hours to a club for teens on the block, which she organized herself. She called it T.H.E.M., for "Trying Hard to Express Myself," she said. She took the young people to plays and movies, bought them books and magazines, gave them scholarships. She brought African Americans successful in many fields, such as politics, publishing, and performing arts, to talk to them. The teens were "not shy" in questioning these role models, Brooks said, nor in challenging her. When Brooks repeatedly spoke of Africa, one of them got disgusted. "Africa this, Africa that," she argued. It's got "nothing at all to do with [us]." Brooks responded by sending the young lady to Ghana, along with another club member and Nora Blakely as chaperone. All the teens repaid her by serving as "watch-workers" protecting the block from crime.[11]

Crime struck Keziah Brooks twice in 1977, when she was nearly ninety. First, on her way home from the grocery store, she was mugged by two young men who snatched her purse. Two other teens, Mrs. Brooks's neighbors, saw the assault

> "It would be very nice if somebody could get some nourishment or healing or just plain rich pleasure out of poems I'm writing today."[12]

and chased the thieves, causing them to drop the pocket-book. Then, one Sunday, while Keziah was out having brunch and shopping with her daughter and son-in-law, her house was broken into and robbed.

Keziah reeled under the violation of her beloved home. She was never the same, Gwendolyn Brooks observed, from that day on.[13] She stopped eating. She became forgetful and vacant. She stopped talking. Gwendolyn took over her mother's care and moved in with her. There seemed to be nothing identifiable wrong, yet Keziah was wasting away.

After a brief hospitalization, she came home to live out her last few weeks. "I am peaceful," she told Gwendolyn. "Thank you."[14] Near the end of Keziah's life, she and her daughter were watching television when a performer began to sing one of Keziah's favorite hymns. Suddenly, the silent old woman began to sing along, and she sang on till the song ended.

When she had to fulfill an out-of-town speaking engagement, Brooks asked Nora Blakely and a professional nurse to take her place. Keziah died quietly with her granddaughter by her side. Nora knew her mother was on her way home from New England by train. She asked the railroad company to deliver an urgent message for Brooks to call home. A conductor relayed the message, and Brooks quickly arranged to fly home.

So deeply did she mourn her mother that Brooks wrote little for the rest of the decade.

Chapter 11

Poet
Laureate

Brooks threw herself into travel and public appearances to work through her sorrow. She toured England and France with a cousin the following summer. She kept up an itinerary of more than fifty college appearances a year for poetry readings and workshops.

She visited Russia (still part of the Communist-ruled Soviet Union at the time) in 1982. Brooks joined American and Soviet authors at a writers' conference aimed at a sharing of views on literature and international friendship. The American delegation then visited historic and cultural sites in the cities of Kiev, Moscow, and Leningrad. Brooks remembered the Russian people's vibrancy, their love of flowers and poetry.

During campus visits, students often asked about her views on race. Brooks was amazed and distressed by a question from an African-American student at Wellesley

College in Massachusetts. "Why do you keep talking about blackness?" the young woman asked. "The time for that is over. We are now Americans, and that is all I want to be."[1]

Once Brooks had discarded this point of view in the sixties, she never reclaimed it. In the Soviet Union, a Russian author had boasted that he never paid attention to another's race. Brooks's answer to him came from her very soul. "Go right ahead and notice that Blacks really look and are quite different from yourself. Go right ahead and PAY ATTENTION," she told him. "Blacks [like me] do not think it would be a blessing if everyone was of the same hue. Personally, I like the idea of a garden rich with varieties of flowers."[2]

Brooks grew tired of being asked so many questions about the black militancy of the 1960s and its poetry.[3] Yet, again, she never changed her mind. "I am consumed with the passion of ideas that I came to believe in in the late sixties. They are now built into myself," she said.[4]

She rebelled when the term "African-American" came to supplant the term "Black" in the 1980s. "I don't like the term African American," she said. "It is very excluding. I like to think of Blacks as family, and the parts of that family that live in Brazil or Haiti or France or England are not going to allow you to call them African American because they are not."[5] She continued to use the term "Black," with a capital B, all her life.

Another question she faced repeatedly was whether blacks and whites would ever be able to live in harmony in the United States. An interviewer noted that she must be optimistic, since she spoke to many white audiences on college campuses. "That's the word for me—optimistic," she replied. "Perhaps because I see so many people, of all kinds . . . that I have faith in people."[6]

Her daughter, Nora Blakely, after graduating from the University of Illinois, pursued various creative careers. She taught school, danced, and choreographed professionally. She had a number of poems published in anthologies, then turned to playwrighting. In 1982, she founded the Chocolate Chip Theatre Company, a Chicago musical and acting troupe. Nora wrote most of their scripts, several of which were based on her mother's work.

Henry Blakely III had moved to California, where he worked as a software developer. He remarried and with his wife presented Brooks with her first grandchild, Nicholas. Brooks proudly described all three of them as "computer expert[s]."[7]

In 1985, Brooks received her most prestigious honor since the Pulitzer Prize. She was named the Library of Congress's consultant in poetry. The next year, the position's title was changed to poet laureate of the United States, which it has remained. At age sixty-eight, she undertook the weekly commute from Chicago to Washington, becoming the most active consultant in years.

Haki Madhubuti

Nora Blakely

Brooks

At a ceremony in Chicago, Brooks holds a portrait
of herself painted by Anne Cressey-McGraw-Beuchamp.

Jacqueline Trescott, a reporter for the *Washington Post*,
interviewed Brooks before her inaugural poetry reading at
the library. Her observations echoed those made so many
years before by writer Frank London Brown. How could
this ordinary-seeming woman be such a powerful, creative
writer? Trescott noted that Brooks wore denim trousers, a
blue head scarf, and senior-citizen shoes. She laughed

Poet Laureate of the United States

The poet laureate consultant in poetry is a spokesperson for the love and enjoyment of reading and writing poetry by ordinary Americans. The poet laureate receives a stipend of $35,000 for the October to May term. The only requirements are to give one lecture and poetry reading, and to introduce visiting poets when they perform their work at the Library of Congress. The consultant has plenty of free time to work on projects of his or her own choosing.

Gwendolyn Brooks was the first African American to be named to this position. She was also the first to work extensively with children, senior citizens, and prisoners.

uproariously, smacking her chair's upholstery so vigorously that the flowers "shimmer[ed]." She could have been "any rider on the bus, any woman in the marketplace," but here she was, "one of America's distinguished poets . . . a vessel of strong ideas," Trescott wrote.[8]

Two hours before the library's auditorium doors opened, an enormous crowd gathered to hear Brooks read. "Euphoria" was the mood of this diverse, multiracial group, said one participant.[9] When the hour arrived, five hundred people were admitted, three hundred watched on video in another room, and another two hundred disappointed fans were turned away. "Oh, Mama," a beaming Nora Blakely told her mother. "It was The Day of the Gwendolyn."[10]

During the year of her residency as consultant in poetry,

Brooks visited dozens of schools. Groups of children came to visit her at the library as well. She described a group that joined her for lunch. "What a time we had. We talked about, not just poetry, but about their grandmothers, about beer, about pizza, and about hair."[11] Brooks also reached out to prisons, drug rehabilitation facilities, and senior citizen centers for her poetry readings. She invited African-American and Hispanic poets to participate in the prestigious Library of Congress lecture series. "You demystified the Library," declared her fellow poet Sonia Sanchez.[12]

In 1987 hundreds of her admirers celebrated Brooks's seventieth birthday. At the annual Illinois Poet Laureate Awards, a group of young award-winners helped her blow out the candles on her cake. Haki Madhubuti planned his own surprise with a commemorative volume of essays by her friends and fellow writers. His own piece praised her as "Queen Mother," one who never "put her art above or before the people she writes about."[13]

Brooks's husband contributed a memoir of their first meeting. Daughter Nora wrote a humorous profile, which dared to reveal "the truth" about the great writer. Her mother, Nora confided, so loved television soap operas that she refused to talk on the telephone when they aired. Once, Nora made the mistake of calling during Brooks's favorite show. Without troubling to find out who was calling, Brooks barked *"All My Children"* into the receiver

Brooks and the Librarian of Congress, Dr. Daniel J. Boorstin.

and slammed the phone down. At other times, she and Nora chatted and giggled away by phone for two or even three hours. And in the mail, Nora daily found letters stuffed with newspaper clippings Brooks thought she should read. "If I take up residence on the moon, the next shuttle will contain clippings from my mother," she joked.[14]

Brooks inherited a concern for nutrition and physical fitness from her mother, who in her eighties had written an essay called "Keziah's Health Book." Gwendolyn exercised along with a television fitness show at 5:30 A.M. daily. Haki Madhubuti had adopted a strict vegetarian diet and urged Brooks to try his regimen. She became a juicing enthusiast, liquefying and drinking a concoction of carrots, green peppers, and spinach every day. But she kept her love of sweets, which he abhorred. "She liked chocolate. She liked fudge," Madhubuti said. Her freezer was "filled with ice cream."[15]

Though he and Nora kept a close eye on the now-elderly couple, the Blakelys mainly took care of themselves. Brooks did her own cooking and cleaning till the end of her life. As her mother's neighborhood had been, Brooks's street was touched by crime. One day, she telephoned Madhubuti in a panic. Someone was trying to break into her house while she was still inside. He dialed 9-1-1, then jumped into his car to race to her side. Fortunately, the thief had been unable to enter and ran off.

During the early 1980s, when grief for her mother had kept her from writing, Brooks published only one book. *To Disembark* was a selection of her best poems since 1967. By the middle of the decade, she had resumed what she called the "delicious agony" of poetry writing.[16] *The Near-Johannesburg Boy and Other Poems* was published in 1986. Topping five hundred pages, the monumental *Blacks*, published in 1987, stood as a testament to Brooks's creative power, containing most of her work up to that point. She continued with *Gottschalk and the Grand Tarantelle* in 1988

Over the years, Brooks published twenty-one volumes
of poetry, one novel, two volumes of autobiography,
and two books on writing poetry.

and *Children Coming Home* in 1991. A second volume of autobiographical sketches, *Report From Part Two*, followed in 1994.

In 1996, the seventy-nine-year-old Henry Blakely died. He "slipped away watching baseball . . . what a way to go," wrote Nikki Giovanni, Brooks's friend and fellow poet.[17] In a memoir of the couple, Giovanni remembered Blakely's amazement on the day his sports-illiterate wife watched a basketball game and even cheered.

Brooks continued to be active and write into her eighties. Shortly before her death from stomach cancer at age eighty-three, she prepared her final book, *In Montgomery and Other Poems*, for publication. She took to her bed only a week before the end. During her last days, Nora Blakely, and Haki Madhubuti and his wife took turns reading to her. On December 3, 2000, she held the hands of her daughter and other friends and passed on.

"When the eulogy is heard and the tributes are given, none of us will have to search for words, bite our tongues or lie," wrote Madhubuti. "We can all tell the truth, she loved us and we loved her."[18]

> "I believe that we should all know each other, we human carriers of so many pleasurable differences. To not know is to doubt, to shrink from, sidestep or destroy."[19]

Chronology

1917—Gwendolyn Elizabeth Brooks born on June 7
     in Topeka, Kansas, and lives in Chicago.

1930—First poem published in a national magazine,
     American Childhood.

1933—Meets James Weldon Johnson and
     Langston Hughes.

1934—Graduates from Englewood High School.

1936—Graduates from Wilson Junior College.

1939—Marries Henry Blakely Jr.

1940—Son Henry Blakely III born.

1941—Takes poetry class from Inez Cunningham Stark.

1943—Wins first Midwestern Writers' Conference
     poetry contest.

1945—*A Street in Bronzeville* is published.

1949—*Annie Allen* is published.

1950—Wins Pulitzer Prize for poetry.

1951—Daughter Nora is born.

1953—*Maud Martha* is published.

1956—*Bronzeville Boys and Girls* is published.

1959—Father David Brooks dies.

1960—*The Bean Eaters* is published.

CHRONOLOGY

1963—*Selected Poems* is published. Begins teaching at Columbia College.

1967—Fisk University Black Writers' Conference.

1968—*In the Mecca* is published. Brooks is named poet laureate of Illinois.

1969—Separates from husband, Henry Blakely.

1970—*Family Pictures* is published.

1971—*The World of Gwendolyn Brooks* is published. Visits Kenya and Tanzania. Suffers minor heart attack.

1972—*Report From Part One* is published.

1974—Reunites with husband. Visits Ghana and England.

1975—*Beckonings* is published.

1976—Brother Raymond Brooks dies.

1978—Mother Keziah Brooks dies.

1981—*To Disembark* is published.

1982—Visits Russia.

1985—Appointed consultant in poetry to the Library of Congress.

1986—*The Near-Johannesburg Boy and Other Poems* is published.

1987—*Blacks* is published.

1991—*Children Coming Home* is published.

1994—Receives the National Book Award Medal for Literature.

1996—Husband dies; *Report From Part Two* is published.

2000—Brooks dies in Chicago on December 4.

Books by Gwendolyn Brooks

Collections

In Montgomery and Other Poems. Chicago: Third World Press, 2003.
> **Includes most of her work from the 1990s.**

Selected Poems. New York: Harper Perennial, 1999.
> **Includes most of her books from Harpers.**

Blacks. Chicago: Third World Press, 1991.
> **Includes most of her work from the 1980s.**

To Disembark. Chicago: Third World Press, 1981.
> **Includes most of her work from the 1970s.**

Complete Works

A Street in Bronzeville, 1945
Annie Allen, 1949
Maud Martha, 1953
Bronzeville Boys and Girls, 1956
The Bean Eaters, 1960
Selected Poems, 1963
In the Mecca, 1968
Riot, 1969
Family Pictures, 1970
Aloneness, 1971
The World of Gwendolyn Brooks, 1971

BOOKS BY GWENDOLYN BROOKS

(Editor) *A Broadside Treasury*, 1971
(Editor) *Jump Bad*, 1971
Report From Part One, 1972
Aurora, 1972
The Tiger Who Wore White Gloves, 1974
Beckonings, 1975
Primer for Blacks, 1980
To Disembark, 1981
Young Poet's Primer, 1981
Black Love, 1982
Mayor Harold Washington [and] Chicago: The I Will City, 1983
Very Young Poets, 1983
The Near Johannesburg Boy, and Other Poems, 1987
Report From Part Two, 1996
In Montgomery, 2001

Chapter Notes

Chapter 1. The Pulitzer Prize

1. Roy Newquist. *Conversations* (Chicago: Rand McNally, 1967), p. 43.

2. *A Conversation With Gwendolyn Brooks* (Library of Congress, 1986), videorecording.

3. Frank Harriott. "The Life of a Pulitzer Poet," *Negro Digest*, August 1950, p. 14.

4. George Kent, *A Life of Gwendolyn Brooks* (Lexington, Ky.: University Press of Kentucky, 1990), p. 116.

5. Harriott, p. 14.

6. Ibid., p. 88.

7. Newquist, p. 43.

8. Harriott, p. 15.

9. Kent, p. 89.

10. Harriott, p. 16.

11. Eloise Perry Hazard. "A Habit of 'Firsts,'" *Saturday Review of Literature*, May 20, 1950, p. 23.

12. Harriott, p. 16.

13. R. Baxter Miller. *Langston Hughes and Gwendolyn Brooks: A Reference Guide.* (Boston: G. K. Hall, 1978), p. 90.

Chapter 2. A Sparkly Childhood

1. Phyllis Garland, "Gwendolyn Brooks: Poet Laureate," *Ebony*, July 1968, p. 49.

2. Gwendolyn Brooks, *Report From Part One* (Detroit, Mich.: Broadside Press, 1972), p. 51.

3. Ibid., p. 52.

4. Gwendolyn Brooks, "Interview," *Triquarterly*, 1984, p. 406.

5. Janet Palmer Mullaney, ed., *Truthtellers of the Times: Interviews with Contemporary Women Poets* (Ann Arbor: University of Michigan Press, 1998), p. 8.

6. Brooks, *Report From Part One*, p. 55.

CHAPTER NOTES

7. Phyllis Garland, "Gwendolyn Brooks: Poet Laureate." *Ebony*, July 1968, p. 52.

8. Claudia Tate, ed., *Black Women Writers at Work* (New York: Continuum, 1983), p. 46.

9. Brooks, *Triquarterly*, p. 405.

10. Brooks, *Report From Part One*, p. 54.

11. George Kent, *A Life of Gwendolyn Brooks* (Lexington, Ky.: University Press of Kentucky, 1990), pp. 16–17.

12. Brooks, *Report From Part One*, p. 38.

13. Ibid., p. 37.

14. Ibid., p. 38.

Chapter 3. "You Have Talent"

1. Phyllis Garland, "Gwendolyn Brooks: Poet Laureate," *Ebony*, July 1968, p. 49.

2. Janet Palmer Mullaney, ed., *Truthtellers of the Times: Interviews with Contemporary Women Poets* (Ann Arbor: University of Michigan Press, 1998), p. 8.

3. Ida Lewis, "Conversation," *Essence*, April 1971, p. 27.

4. Garland, p. 50.

5. George Kent, *A Life of Gwendolyn Brooks* (Lexington, Ky.: University Press of Kentucky, 1990), p. 19.

6. Garland, p. 50. Also in Kent, pp. 19–22.

7. Gwendolyn Brooks, *Report From Part One* (Detroit: Broadside Press, 1972), p. 57.

8. Gwendolyn Brooks, *Report From Part Two* (Chicago: Third World Press, 1996), p. 13.

9. B. Denise Hawkins, "An Evening With Gwendolyn Brooks," *Black Issues in Higher Education*, November 3, 1994, p. 21.

10. Brooks, *Report From Part One*, p. 56.

11. Roy Newquist, *Conversations* (Chicago: Rand McNally, 1967), p. 38.

12. Brooks, *Report From Part One*, p. 56.

13. Ibid., p. 202.

14. *A Conversation With Gwendolyn Brooks* (Library of Congress, 1986), videorecording. Brooks told this story many

times. See other versions in Garland, p. 50; *Report From Part One*, p. 173; and *Report From Part Two*, p. 11.

15. Garland, p. 50.

16. *A Conversation With Gwendolyn Brooks.*

17. Kent, p. 19.

18. Brooks, *Report From Part One*, p. 57.

Chapter 4. Daughter of the Dusk

1. Ida Lewis, "Conversation," *Essence*, April 1971, p. 28.

2. Ibid.

3. Ibid.

4. George Kent, *A Life of Gwendolyn Brooks* (Lexington, Ky.: University Press of Kentucky, 1990), pp. 27–28.

5. Ibid., p. 31.

6. B. Denise Hawkins, "An Evening With Gwendolyn Brooks," *Black Issues in Higher Education*, November 3, 1994, p. 20.

7. Kent, p. 27.

8. Phyllis Garland, "Gwendolyn Brooks: Poet Laureate," *Ebony*, July 1968, p. 52. See also Kent, p. 41.

9. Roy Newquist, *Conversations* (Chicago: Rand McNally, 1967), p. 38. See also Garland, p. 52.

10. Gwendolyn Brooks, *Report From Part One* (Detroit: Broadside Press, 1972), p. 190.

11. Newquist, p. 39.

12. Garland, p. 53.

13. Newquist, p. 39. See also Brooks, *Report From Part One*, p. 58.

Chapter 5. Wife, Mother, Poet

1. Haki R. Madhubuti, ed., *Say That the River Turns: The Impact of Gwendolyn Brooks* (Chicago: Third World Press, 1987), p. 6.

2. Ibid.

3. George Kent, *A Life of Gwendolyn Brooks* (Lexington, Ky.: University Press of Kentucky, 1990), p. 45.

4. Madhubuti, p. 5.

5. Kent, p. 45.

CHAPTER NOTES

6. Gwendolyn Brooks, *Report From Part One* (Detroit: Broadside Press, 1972), p. 59.

7. Kent, p. 53.

8. Roy Newquist, *Conversations* (Chicago: Rand McNally, 1967), p. 41.

9. Ida Lewis, "Conversation," *Essence*, April 1971, p. 30.

10. Kent, p. 38.

11. Brooks, p. 59.

12. Newquist, p. 40.

13. Eloise Perry Hazard. "A Habit of 'Firsts,'" *Saturday Review of Literature*, May 20, 1950, p. 23.

14. Lewis, p. 29.

15. Newquist, p. 41.

16. Ibid.

Chapter 6. Portrait of Bronzeville

1. Phyllis Garland, "Gwendolyn Brooks: Poet Laureate," *Ebony*, July 1968, p. 54.

2. George Kent, *A Life of Gwendolyn Brooks* (Lexington, Ky.: University Press of Kentucky, 1990), p. 63.

3. Roy Newquist, *Conversations* (Chicago: Rand McNally, 1967), p. 42.

4. L. S. Dembo and Cyrena N. Pondrom, eds., *The Contemporary Writer*, Madison, Wisc.: University of Wisconsin Press, 1972), p. 239.

5. Mel Watkins, "Gwendolyn Brooks (1917–2000)," *Black Scholar*, Spring 2001, p. 51.

6. Newquist, p. 42.

7. Ibid.

8. Gwendolyn Brooks, *Report From Part One* (Detroit: Broadside Press, 1972), p. 72.

9. Ibid.

10. Garland, p. 54.

11. Jacqueline Crockett, "An Essay on Gwendolyn Brooks," *Negro History Bulletin*, November 1955, p. 38.

12. Kent, p. 64.

13. Juliette Bowles, ed., *In the Memory and Spirit of Frances, Zora, and Lorraine: Essays and Interviews on Black Women and*

Writing (Atlanta: Institute for Arts and Humanities, Howard University, 1979), p. 2.

14. "*Black Books Bulletin* Interviews: Gwendolyn Brooks," *Black Books Bulletin*, Spring 1974, p. 34.

15. Brooks, p. 70.

16. Kent, p. 77.

17. Ibid.

18. Langston Hughes, *The Collected Works of Langston Hughes, Volume 9* (Columbia, Mo.: University of Missouri Press, 2002), p. 537.

19. Phyllis McGinley, "Poetry for Prose Readers," *New York Times Book Review*, January 22, 1950, p. 7.

20. Brooks, p. 214.

21. Sheldon Hackney, "A Conversation With Gwendolyn Brooks," *Humanities*, May/June 1994, p. 4.

22. Kent, p. 92.

Chapter 7. "Poets Who Are Negroes"

1. George Kent, *A Life of Gwendolyn Brooks* (Lexington, Ky.: University Press of Kentucky, 1990), p. 95.

2. Ibid., p. 89.

3. Gwendolyn Brooks, "Poets Who Are Negroes," *Phylon*, Fourth Quarter 1950, p. 312.

4. Ida Lewis, "Conversation," *Essence*, April 1971, p. 30.

5. Langston Hughes, ed., Foreword by Gwendolyn Brooks, *New Negro Poets, U.S.A.* (Bloomington, Ind.: Indiana University Press, 1964), p. 13.

6. Kent, p. 104.

7. Gwendolyn Brooks, *Report From Part Two* (Chicago: Third World Press, 1996), p. 28.

8. Hubert Creekmore, "Maud Martha," *New York Times Book Review*, October 4, 1953, p. 4.

9. Coleman Rosenberger, "A Work of Art and Jeweled Precision," *New York Herald-Tribune Book Review*, October 18, 1953, p. 4.

10. Gwendolyn Brooks, "Interview," *Triquarterly*, 1984, p. 408.

11. Gwendolyn Brooks, *Report From Part One* (Detroit: Broadside Press, 1972), p. 60.

12. Ibid.

13. Ibid., p. 209.

14. Kent, p. 118.

15. Roy Newquist, *Conversations* (Chicago: Rand McNally, 1967), p. 45.

16. *A Conversation With Gwendolyn Brooks* (Library of Congress, 1986), videorecording.

17. Herbert Burke, "The Bean Eaters," *Library Journal*, April 15, 1960, p. 1599.

18. L.S. Dembo and Cyrena N. Pondrom, eds., *The Contemporary Writer* (Madison, Wisc.: University of Wisconsin Press, 1972) pp. 250–251.

Chapter 8. Time of the Tall Walkers

1. Frank London Brown, "Chicago's Great Lady of Poetry," *Negro Digest*, December 1961, p. 54.

2. George Kent, *A Life of Gwendolyn Brooks* (Lexington, Ky.: University Press of Kentucky, 1990), pp. 148–149.

3. Roy Newquist, *Conversations* (Chicago: Rand McNally, 1967), p. 43.

4. Gwendolyn Brooks, *Report From Part One* (Detroit: Broadside Press, 1972), p. 62.

5. Langston Hughes, ed., *New Negro Poets U.S.A.* (Bloomington, Ind.: Indiana University Press, 1964), p. 13.

6. Ibid.

7. Brooks, p. 198.

8. Ibid., pp. 189–190.

9. Ibid., p. 84.

10. Ida Lewis, "Conversation: Gwen Brooks 'My People Are Black People,'" *Essence*, April 1971, p. 27.

11. Claudia Tate, ed., *Black Women Writers at Work* (New York: Continuum, 1983), p. 40.

12. Brooks, p. 85.

13. Tate, p. 40.

14. Gwendolyn Brooks, Keorapetse Kgositsile, Haki R. Madhubuti, and Dudley Randall, *A Capsule Course in Black Poetry Writing* (Detroit, Mich.: Broadside Press, 1975), pp. 4–5.

Chapter 9. Into the Whirlwind

1. George Kent, *A Life of Gwendolyn Brooks* (Lexington, Ky.: University Press of Kentucky, 1990), p. 203.

2. Claudia Tate, ed., *Black Women Writers at Work* (New York: Continuum, 1983), p. 40.

3. Ida Lewis, "Conversation: Gwen Brooks 'My People Are Black People,'" *Essence*, April 1971, p. 27.

4. Tate, p. 40.

5. Patrick T. Reardon. "Remembering 'Gwen' a Personal Memoir of Gwendolyn Brooks from the Late Poet Laureate's Library 'Son,'" *Chicago Tribune*, December 8, 2000, p. 1.

6. "*Black Books Bulletin* Interviews: Gwen Brooks," June 1974, p. 30. See also Lewis, p. 27, and Tate, pp. 40–41.

7. Phyllis Garland, "Gwendolyn Brooks: Poet Laureate," *Ebony*, July 1968, p. 49.

8. Ibid., p. 56.

9. Reardon, p. 1.

10. Lewis, p. 30.

11. Gwendolyn Brooks, *Report From Part One* (Detroit: Broadside Press, 1972), p. 45.

12. Tate, p. 41.

13. Lewis, p. 29.

14. D. H. Melhem, *Heroism in the New Black Poetry: Introductions & Interviews* (Lexington, Ky: University Press of Kentucky, 1990), p. 18.

15. Brooks, p. 21.

16. Ibid., p. 206.

17. Gwendolyn Brooks, *Jump Bad: A New Chicago Anthology* (Detroit: Broadside Press, 1971), p. 12.

18. Reardon, p. 1.

19. Kent, pp. 223–224.

20. Brooks, p. 58.

CHAPTER NOTES

Chapter 10. Furious Flower

1. Gwendolyn Brooks, *Report From Part One* (Detroit: Broadside Press, 1972), p. 58.

2. Gloria T. Hull and Posey Gallagher, "Update on Part One: An Interview With Gwendolyn Brooks," *CLA Journal*, September 1977, p. 35.

3. George Kent, *A Life of Gwendolyn Brooks* (Lexington, Ky.: University Press of Kentucky, 1990), p. 240.

4. Brooks, p. 88.

5. D. H. Melhem, *Heroism in the New Black Poetry: Introductions & Interviews* (Lexington, Ky: University Press of Kentucky, 1990), p. 11.

6. Ibid.

7. Hull and Gallagher, p. 30.

8. Gwendolyn Brooks, *Report From Part Two* (Chicago: Third World Press, 1996), p. 48.

9. Hull and Gallagher, p. 35.

10. "A Local Legacy: An Interview with Nora Brooks Blakely by Sharon Bloyd-Peshkin," *Chicago Parent online*, n.d., <http://www.chicagoparent.com/CP_pages/archive/Interview%20Archive/Int0101.htm> (November 28, 2003).

11. Gwendolyn Brooks, "Interview," *Triquarterly*, 1984, p. 409.

12. Steve Cape, "An Interview With Gwendolyn Brooks," Artful Dodge, College of Wooster, Ohio, n.d., <http://www.wooster.edu/artfuldodge/interviews/brooks.htm> (September 20, 2004).

13. Brooks, *Report From Part Two*, p. 23.

14. Ibid., p. 40.

Chapter 11. Poet Laureate

1. Janet Palmer Mullaney, ed., *Truthtellers of the Times: Interviews with Contemporary Women Poets* (Ann Arbor: University of Michigan Press, 1998), p. 9.

2. Gwendolyn Brooks, "Black Woman in Russia," *Humanities*, May/June 1994, p. 28.

3. Sheldon Hackney, "A Conversation With Gwendolyn Brooks," *Humanities*, May/June 1994, p. 7.

4. Gloria T. Hull and Posey Gallagher, "Update on Part One: An Interview With Gwendolyn Brooks," *CLA Journal*, September 1977, p. 25.

5. B. Denise Hawkins, "An Evening With Gwendolyn Brooks," *Black Issues in Higher Education*, November 3, 1994, p. 21.

6. Martha Satz, "Honest Reporting: An Interview With Gwendolyn Brooks," *Southwest Review*, Winter 1989, p. 29.

7. Gwendolyn Brooks, *Report From Part Two* (Chicago: Third World Press, 1996), p. 163.

8. Jacqueline Trescott, "The 40-Year Quest of the Poet," *Washington Post*, September 25, 1985, p. D1.

9. Mullaney, p. 11.

10. Brooks, p. 76.

11. *A Conversation With Gwendolyn Brooks* (Library of Congress, 1986), videorecording.

12. Brooks, p. 84.

13. Haki R. Madhubuti, ed., *Say That the River Turns: The Impact of Gwendolyn Brooks* (Chicago: Third World Press, 1987), p. xii.

14. Ibid., p. 7.

15. Patrick T. Reardon, "Remembering 'Gwen' a Personal Memoir of Gwendolyn Brooks from the Late Poet Laureate's Liberary 'Son,'" *Chicago Tribune*, December 8, 2000, p. 1.

16. Hackney, p. 4.

17. Nikki Giovanni, "No Complaints for Gwendolyn Brooks. . . ," *Black Collegian*, April 2001, p. 99.

18. Haki R. Madhubuti, "Gwendolyn Brooks (1917–2000)," *Black Issues in Higher Education*, December 21, 2000, p. 15.

19. "Gwendolyn Brooks, 83, Who Won Pulitzer Prize for Poetry, Dies," *Jet*, December 18, 2000, p. 18.

Further Reading

For Middle School Students

Bloom, Harold. *Gwendolyn Brooks*.
  Philadelphia: Chelsea House, 2004.

Strickland, Michael. *African-American Poets*.
  Berkeley Heights, N.J.: Enslow Publishers, Inc., 1996.

Wheeler, Jill C. *Gwendolyn Brooks*. Edina, Minn.: Abdo, 1997.

For High School Students

Brooks, Gwendolyn. *Report From Part One*.
  Detroit: Broadside Press, 1972.

Brooks, Gwendolyn. *Report From Part Two*.
  Chicago: Third World Press, 1996.

Giles, Gloria Wade, ed. *Conversations With Gwendolyn
  Brooks*. Jackson: University Press of Mississippi, 2003.

Kent, George. *A Life of Gwendolyn Brooks*. Lexington, Ky.:
  The University Press of Kentucky, 1990.

Melhem, D. H. *Gwendolyn Brooks: Poetry and the Heroic Voice*.
  Lexington, Ky.: The University Press of Kentucky, 1987.

Internet Addresses

American Academy of Poets' Gwendolyn Brooks Page
  <http://www.poets.org/poet.php/prmPID/165>

Gwendolyn Brooks Teacher Resource File
  <http://falcon.jmu.edu/~ramseyil/brooks.htm>

University of Illinois's Modern American Poetry Web site
  **<http://www.english.uiuc.edu/maps/poets/a_f/
  brooks/brooks.htm>**

Index

Page numbers for photographs are in **boldface** type.

INDEX